DRAGGING and DRIVING

by Tom MacPherson

Illustrated with line drawings by Denny McMains

WILDSIDE PRESS

ACKNOWLEDGMENTS

The author and artist are grateful to the following for their help in preparing this book:

Mrs. Robert Koenig, R. N., for reviewing the section on first aid.

Mr. Richard Horton, Ford Motor Company, for supplying material useful in preparing illustrations.

Creepers Auto Club of Jamesburg, N. J.

Automotive Crash Injury Research of Cornell University, National Hot Rod Association, American Trucking Associations, Chrysler Corporation, and the Teen-Age Road-e-o Committee of the U. S. Junior Chamber of Commerce.

CONTENTS

1. Two-Way Ticket 1
2. Buying Your First Car 8
3. Backyard Customizing 18
4. The Real Rail Job 37
5. Getting into Competition 46
6. So You're Stuck with the Stock 53
7. How to be Chicken and Popular 65
8. Skids, Skins, and Skills 78
9. Had an Accident? 90
10. Second Impact 113
11. Tomorrow's Driving 124
Appendix I, Dragging Jargon 135
Appendix II, What Makes It Go? 145
Index 153

1. Two-Way Ticket

ON THE DAY you reach the legal minimum age at which you can hold a driver's license you will probably have spent two thirds of your life absorbing a philosophy completely contrary to good driving.

We begin to absorb that philosophy in our early school days. First we are urged merely to "do better," to compete against a system of grades. Then we are needled to shoot for the "A." Somewhere along the line we meet the honor roll, and as the roll is for the top students of each class, we are now fighting to be first. At home we get more prodding to be aggressive; someone tells us, "Eddie Jones can make honor roll and *you're smarter* than he is."

Soon there is our team in interclass baseball. If we

don't make the team, we're out there rooting: Win! Win! Win! During gym period there are relay races, mat wrestling, rope climbing, and a lot of competitive games. We're right in there, giving our all to win, or cheering our team or our buddy on to victory.

We get into high school and the crescendo really builds up. Now we are competing against outlanders—teams from other schools—baseball, football, basketball, wrestling in most schools, boxing in a few. We're saturated with the aggressive spirit. Make the team! Be a cheerleader, or at least get out to the game and scream for victory. Mow down the other team!

By the second day in high school we have learned that only the top few students will have their choice of college. Many of us are told that college entrance boards also look into our leadership qualities, and leadership is a quality of the extrovert, the aggressive type. This is the mounting pressure for individual triumph: top honors . . . valuable scholarships . . . class president . . . valedictorian . . . be the best; be the utmost.

Then comes the day when, by virtue of a birth certificate and a short road test, we are eligible to pilot three thousand pounds of mechanical energy on public roads. Perhaps nobody tells us so, but now we must throw an entire philosophy into reverse. This is where we separate real drivers from the kids. The competitive and aggressive driver is a misfit on the highway. You don't win at highway roulette by being aggressive. If the other driver is bent on crashing the line, let him. You survive by being defensive, by not slamming into a charging offensive. Sooner or later the aggressive driver scores a tie. Unlike football, a tie on the road means all losers, no winners.

Your first driving license is a two-way ticket for which you have practiced and waited for months, maybe years. Now that you finally have it, you have a ticket to pleasant, exciting, and perhaps profitable years. It may be your ticket to many or all the outside activities of your school, to the senior class play, to the football and basketball games played away from home field. It's a ticket to dances and swimming parties and to other social events which nondrivers must sometimes pass up. In short, your driving license is your ticket to fun and popularity.

It is a ticket, too, to that part-time job which might otherwise be beyond your reach, for some jobs have the annoying habit of being located on the wrong bus route. It is a ticket that could possibly decide which college you attend; for some colleges have limited student housing, and your car may be your only dependable means of transportation.

It's a durable ticket. It takes from one to three years to expire, depending upon where you live. When it does expire, you can renew it for not more than a few dollars each time. In a few states a driver's license never expires, except when the driver kills it for himself.

Your driver's license is also a ticket to responsibility. It is perhaps the first formal recognition you get from an adult society that you are no longer a kid. It may be a few years before you are legally an adult and entitled to vote, but the law now recognizes that you are mature enough to control a surging combustible chariot on public roads and crowded city streets. Your driver's license makes you responsible for the life of every person who steps into or in front of the vehicle you are driving or who occupies another vehicle sharing the roads with you.

That responsibility is the main reason why one item listed on your license is important to many people. That item is your age. Your age is watched closely by statisticians who compile the data on automobile accidents. One unhappy statistic they keep coming up with is that the very young and the very old have the largest share of accidents. Your age is important, too, to the insurance actuaries, the men who determine insurance rates. They have never seen you or heard of you personally, but they had you written down as a bad risk as soon as you received your first license. Before you even begin to drive, you are a bad insurance risk strictly because of the record of other drivers your age.

Finally, your age is important financially to your own family. If you are the only male driver under twenty-five in the family, you know that your license has taken a big bite out of the family treasury. Liability insurance on the family car was automatically hiked up when you got that license. If you are going to drive your own car instead of the family car, the insurance cost is even greater. Unfortunately, that is the way it is going to be until you reach your twenty-fifth birthday. The insurance picture will get better before that only when next year's teen-agers demonstrate that they are less aggressive drivers than last year's crop.

It takes most of us too long to cotton to the idea of defensive driving. We are reluctant to give up the idea of winning. We compete for the fastest getaway as soon as the light turns green. We try to outbluff the other driver at intersections. We hate to get passed by other cars on the highway. These are the kid-stuff reasons why single men under twenty-five, though they represent only 14 per cent of all drivers, are involved in 30 per cent of the accidents.

Accidents mean injured people and damaged automobiles. Hospitalization and automotive repairs are expensive. And so the insurance actuaries have ruled that the group of drivers who account for double the average rate of accidents must pay double the average rate of insurance. The arithmetic may not be quite as simple as that, but that is the general philosophy of automobile liability insurance.

Insurance rates favor the older, experienced driver because his experience has curbed his aggressiveness and made him a defensive driver. The defensive driver is neither chicken nor a loser.

He's the survivor. He knows his defensive driving means he will stand a better chance of escaping fender wrinkling or worse damage. He knows that both drivers in an accident usually have some responsibility even though one has the legal right of way. He always honors the responsibility portion of his two-way ticket and that is his best insurance for continuing to enjoy the portion that brings him fun and profit.

Like any seasoned traveler, the good driver knows you only get your money's worth out of a two-way ticket by using the return portion. That's a thought which you can chew on from a few different angles.

Three Peeks at the Back

As you go through this book you are going to have questions on how some things work . . . what some screwball words mean . . . where some gismo on an automobile engine is located. The answers are in the book, though they won't always be on the same page your eyes are when the question pops into your mind. To help you find answers fast, there are three sections at the back of the book where you can check.

First, a glossary of words used by hot rodders and other automobile men. The glossary is titled "Dragging Jargon," and you will find it on page 135.

Second, a diagram of a typical automobile engine, with detailed explanations of how the different engine parts function. See "What Makes It Go" on page 145.

Finally, the index. Whether your question is "What does the Johnson rod do?" or just "Where is the Johnson rod?" the index will tell you on which page to look for the answer.

2. Buying Your First Car

Your first car may be the one "she" you will be dating the steadiest for the longest. She will most likely be a used car, and may represent your earnings from one or more summer jobs. If you intend to customize your car, you will be pouring most of your future income and pocket money into it and so you won't save much toward buying a better model next year. That means that unless you are lucky enough to rate a new car or to inherit the family's second-best buggy, you just have to get the most and best automobile for your money the first time you invest in a used vehicle.

It is fairly easy to tell what a man is interested in when he inspects the latest models in an automobile dealer's showroom. He is interested in a new car.

Buying Your First Car 9

But in a used-car lot you can't always tell whether the visitor is interested in a car or in an excuse to buy new shoes for himself. You know the type we mean—the one who approaches an auto, kicks the tires, then walks over to another car.

The best method, possibly the only method, of getting your full money's worth is to inspect and test a used car thoroughly, using steps which have themselves been fully tested. Points to examine are explained in the following pages. Unless you have enough automotive savvy to remember all these points, don't be ashamed to make a list of them and to refer to the list when you are looking over a used car.

It is quite reasonable to test a used car, and most dealers expect their customers to do so. But unless you know what you are doing you automatically make yourself an easy mark for any glib salesman who spots you as a phony. On the other hand, if you know the correct procedure for testing a used vehicle, the dealer who is honest about the condition of his merchandise will gladly let you inspect any automobile thoroughly.

You will undoubtedly decide what make and model of car you would like to own before you have reached the legal driving age or before you have accumulated enough green stuff for the down payment. This early decision gives you time for window shopping. Scout all the used-car dealers in the area in which you expect to do your real shopping. Note the cars in each lot and try to remember those that stay there a long time. Note particularly those that come back after a short absence from the lot. Don't be the next unhappy owner of a lemon.

By checking used-car lots in this manner you may also become useful to the family should the folks find themselves in the market for a used car. Whether for the family or for yourself, once you are ready to buy a car be firm about the complete inspection and test of any car you are seriously considering. But don't be the nuisance type who gives the full treatment to every car on the lot even though he knew before he walked in that he was interested in one or two specific models.

It's okay to take a friend with you who has real mechanical knowledge, but not someone who merely talks like an expert. Automobile salesmen can have only two objections to your giving a car a thorough going over. One objection may be that they do not believe you are serious about buying, and a companion who clowns or who runs down each car with a flow of corny wisecracks will strengthen that belief. The other objection may be that the car won't stand up under close inspection. If you are serious about buying, you should not have much trouble convincing the dealer. If he is convinced you are serious but still discourages a close inspection of the car, your best course is to look at another car, preferably in another dealer's lot.

Walk around the car and inspect the body for obvious marks. A dent here and there won't signify much. A long crease that has been touched up, or a door or fender of obviously different shade from the rest of the car, could mean the car has been banged hard. Look for highlights or reflections on the top or sides of the body; they are easier to notice in bright daylight. If you notice repainted areas or bubbled spots on the surface, try to estimate how big an area is affected. These clues—highlights, reflections, and bubbled areas—might be evidence that the car has been badly damaged. It could be still out of line or riding on a sprung chassis. Head for another car. A car with a sprung chassis or wheels out of line burns up tires and is sometimes difficult to control. You can seldom predict which way it will skid when you are forced to hit your brakes suddenly.

Run your fingers along the lower edges—doors, fenders, and bottom chrome strips—applying pressure as you do so. Flaking paint, bubbled surfaces, or rust spots may indicate there is extensive body rusting which is not visible to the eye.

Manipulate the door and window handles to find out whether they operate smoothly and are firmly in place. If the door sags when you open it and has to be slammed before it will close, that may be a sign of a bent frame.

Never take the mileage figure on the odometer for granted. It can be turned back too easily. There's no sure way of telling the exact mileage of a car, but there are telltale signs that will let you know whether the odometer figure reads lower than it should. Armrests, seat covers, floor mats, and pedals that are badly worn indicate much use. Much use means much mileage. If any of those items are new, that probably means the old ones they replaced must have been well worn.

New seat covers may mean, of course, that the previous owner was fastidious. They may also mean that the seat upholstery is soiled or worn or damaged. Prod the surface of the seats to see whether they sag or whether any springs are broken. Do this regardless of the age or condition of the seat covers.

Press down the brake pedal and maintain pressure on it for thirty or forty seconds. If the pedal sinks steadily toward the floor there is leakage in the hydraulic brake system.

If the car has a clutch, press it down with your finger tips. It should go down freely for about one inch before engaging. If the pedal does not go down freely this is an indication that the clutch is considerably worn and has been raised to give as much service as possible before it folds up completely.

Test the steering wheel with a light finger grip. A little free play before the front wheels turn is okay. More than two inches of play is too much. On a car equipped with power steering there should be no play in the steering wheel while the engine is running.

If you are still interested in this particular car after getting this far, you are ready to look under the hood. Get the salesman to disconnect the starter motor at the distributor cap so that you can test the starter. Operate it briefly five or six times. If it grinds or clanks there may be teeth worn or missing on the starter flywheel.

Hook up the distributor again and start the engine, keeping the hood open. An untrained ear may not be able to detect all flaws by listening to the motor, but if there is a damaged cylinder the noise may be a giveaway. Look for other obvious flaws —the fan chewing the radiator, or water or oil seeping through the head and other connections. While the engine is running test the windshield wipers, horn, lights, turn signals, and all the other powered accessories necessary for safe and legal driving.

Watch the exhaust pipe while someone races the engine. A thick blue smoke may mean the car needs a ring job; that's expensive. Before shutting off the engine, check the dashboard instruments. Note whether the battery, oil, and temperature gauges are registering. (Unfortunately, an "improvement" in most late-model cars has been the elimination of actual gauges. You merely get a "trouble light" on the dashboard when a car is too hot, or the battery is not charging, or the oil is low. On some models, all these lights glow momentarily when you turn on the ignition; that may be your only method of checking whether they are functioning.) While at the dash, try the directional signals again, this time checking the light or clicker that is supposed to let you know when the signals are working properly.

If the tires are worn smooth (look at the spare, too) you can figure that the price of a new set adds that much to the cost of the car. Consider, too, that thoroughly worn tires mean the car has traveled a minimum of 20,000 miles. If you are being offered a late-model, low-mileage car, compare the tire wear with the odometer reading. Tires seldom wear evenly, but extremely uneven wear may mean that the front wheels need to be aligned.

Now, squat beside one front wheel in approximately the position you would take to change a flat tire. Hold the tire firmly at the top with both hands and push and pull at it. If it gives easily or makes metallic noises, that's bad. It means worn wheel bearings or suspension parts, and they are expensive to repair.

If you are satisfied with the car up to this point ask for a road test. If the dealer says "no," start thinking about looking at another car in a different lot. If you are asked to put up a deposit, make sure you get a receipt and that it specifies that you get your deposit returned in cash if you reject the car. The dealer may want you to leave the deposit as credit toward another car. Don't agree to that.

Ask the salesman to let you do the test driving, provided, of course, you have a driver's license. If he insists on driving himself, that is reasonable, but get him to operate all the different controls. Listen to the transmission for sounds of faulty operation. Make several starts from an idling stop and check on whether the clutch engages smoothly and without grinding or jerking. Be sure you try reverse gear.

With the car moving forward at 10 mph, accelerate it to 45 and see whether it increases speed without engine hesitation or bucking. If the transmission is automatic, the car should shift smoothly. An engine that races itself between automatic shifts is warning you of trouble.

Test the brakes with several stops, each time braking harder than the last time. Use the same moderate speed each time. Stops should be smooth, with the car still pointing in the exact direction in which it was traveling. If the car swerves to one side or the brakes make loud screeching noises, the brakes may need relining or replacing. If the brake pedal works all the way down to the floor, then either the brake shoes are thin or the fluid is low or leaking.

On a straight road without a center crown, set the car on a straight course and relax your grip on the steering wheel without fully removing your hands. If the car pulls consistently to the same side it could mean that the front end is defective. If there is a cross wind on the road, try riding in both directions before deciding whether the pull is in the car or in the force of the wind.

Find a rough, curving road and listen for rattles and squeaks. Each noise indicates something which may need adjusting or tightening, or is already beyond adjusting. The more noises, the worse the general body condition of the vehicle. While traveling the rough road notice whether the steering is jerky and whether the front end wobbles considerably after striking a bump. These are both signs that expensive front-end repair work is needed.

After your test ride open the hood to see whether there is any evidence of grease or other packing in the head or cylinder block. Next, walk around a bit, breathing deeply to clear odors from your head; then sit in the front seat again and sniff for signs of seeping oil or gasoline.

Finally, if your state requires that automobiles be inspected, ask the salesman if the sale of the car is conditional upon its passing the road inspection. If his answer is "yes," try to get that condition included in your contract to buy the car. If his answer is "no," then don't buy the car. If the dealer decided before you came along that the car was not worth putting in shape to pass the state inspection, then it certainly is a bad investment for you.

Some of the tactics used by a shrewd buyer who is shopping for a new car may also be applied in bargaining for a used car. Timing, for instance. Buy toward the last few days of the month. If the dealer has already done enough business to cover his expenses for that month he may be more inclined to shave the price a little. Buy during the winter, preferably when there is a spell of foul weather. Few cars are sold at such times, so the dealer has more time for you and more desire to sell you a car.

What about used foreign models? They are

sporty, yes, and many foreign cars are cheaper to run than American sixes and eights. But, unless you are an automotive mechanic and metalsmith (and can custom-forge parts when you need them), you run the risk of being grounded for weeks or months while waiting for repairs for your car. There are a few exceptions, but parts for foreign cars, especially body parts, are hard to find. This is also true, unfortunately, of some makes whose importers advertise the existence of parts supply depots located throughout the country.

The best insurance against getting a lemon in a used car is to buy from a dealer with a good reputation. His price may at first seem higher than the prices advertised by flashier agencies, but once you have tried to buy the "specials" at the advertised prices you will come around to the conclusion that it is sometimes rash to believe everything you read in the papers.

Finally, don't ever be talked into taking any vehicle unless you yourself are wholeheartedly sold on it. You are going to foot the bills for gas and maintenance. Foot those bills for a car of your own choice.

3. Backyard Customizing

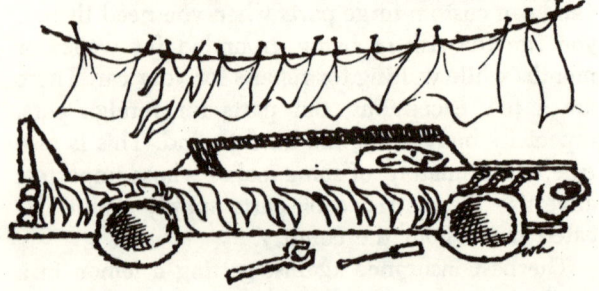

THE AVERAGE HOT ROD is a twice-created vehicle. It was built on a Detroit assembly line one or more years ago, then substantially rebuilt to one individual's taste sometime later. The rebuilding process is almost continuous and may cost the owner the same amount of money as a recent Detroit model would cost him.

That is the average hot rod. As with all averages, there are few or no specific examples that hit the average on the nose. There are countless examples below and above it. Far above the average hot rod, and beyond the reach of the average bankroll, is the "rail job." The rail job is strictly for competition. It is a vehicle that costs its owner several thousand dollars, and one that he will not drive

Backyard Customizing

on the streets for two reasons: one, he has built it and nurtured it specifically for drag racing and cannot afford to impair its efficiency; two, the law would never allow the vehicle on public roads anyway.

On the under side of the average is the rod customized in the family garage, driveway, or backyard. You start with a vehicle that has six to ten years of road wear behind it. If you are either canny or lucky your investment at this point can be considered to be low. Canniness will get you a stock car in reasonably good running condition for less than $300. Luck might get you the family's castoff vehicle when the folks decide to plunge on a brand-new job.

Assuming that the vehicle is your own, to do with as you please (within law and reason), and it pleases you to convert it into a hot rod, you can rework either the motor or the body, or both. If you elect to limit your customizing to the body you can change the silhouette and appearance of your car for as little as four dollars, or you can spend several times the original cash value of the vehicle on flashy additions. On your first customizing operation you will probably spend a sum between these extremes and after that you will keep altering the rod as the mood and the money come to you. If you decide to soup up your motor and make no alterations in the body, you probably won't get by for as little as four dollars. On the other hand, you can pretty much rebuild your entire power plant and yet not spend as much as you might if you went hog wild on the body.

Once you go beyond minor alterations or adjustments, you will find that some of the work must be done in a garage or machine shop. No matter how high your mechanical skill, it is not likely that you will have ready access to the power and pneumatic tools that some parts of the job will require. On the other hand, no matter how low your mechanical knowledge when you start out, you can still handle the simple part of the job and save yourself money. For instance, it is both reasonable and wise to pay to have an experienced mechanic mill the head, but it is downright foolish to pay a mechanic's hourly rate ($4.00 or more) for the unskilled work of removing all the working parts that are connected to the head. The same general principle applies to customizing the body; you can strip chrome off the body with your own hands or add decals and so on, but chopping door posts to lower the roof is work for a trained body man.

Now, just what can you do and what can you not do yourself? Assuming that you have no automotive skill beyond knowing the working ends of three basic tools—screwdriver, wrench, and pliers—here is what you can do yourself to motor and body, and what you should get a skilled mechanic to do. If you *know* you can do more than the unskilled work, do it and save a little money. If you *think* you can do more on your own, don't; take it to the mechanic and save a lot of money.

Souping Up the Engine

Few standard-size automobiles on used-car lots today go beyond a compression ratio of 10 to 1. Most of them are between 9.6 to 1 and 8 to 1. The compact American cars and foreign small cars run between 8.5 to 1 and 6.6 to 1.

"Compression" is the degree of power the drive shaft gets out of each firing of each cylinder. Keeping the compression ratio down gets safety and longer wear out of the engine. Raising the compression ratio results in more power and some gasoline economy. The "economy" is insignificant, and not worth serious consideration. You really up your compression ratio mainly because it is the least expensive alteration that will produce more zip—more horsepower. It is usually safe to increase the ratio of the average stock engine to as much as 11 to 1, but only if you are willing to pay for premium gasoline and never burn the regular grade.

One of the most popular, comparatively inexpensive ways to up your compression ratio is to "mill the head." This means shaving a fraction of the thickness off the bottom of the head so that the cylinder chambers are just a little smaller than they were when the engine was manufactured. Inside the smaller chambers the gas and air mixture, being compressed that much more, exerts a more powerful force when exploded by the firing of the spark plug.

Milling a head is no job for the backyard mechanic. It is strictly a machine-shop job, since the

REMOVING THE HEAD, OVERHEAD VALVE V-8
THUNDERBIRD 292 CU. IN. DISPLACEMENT

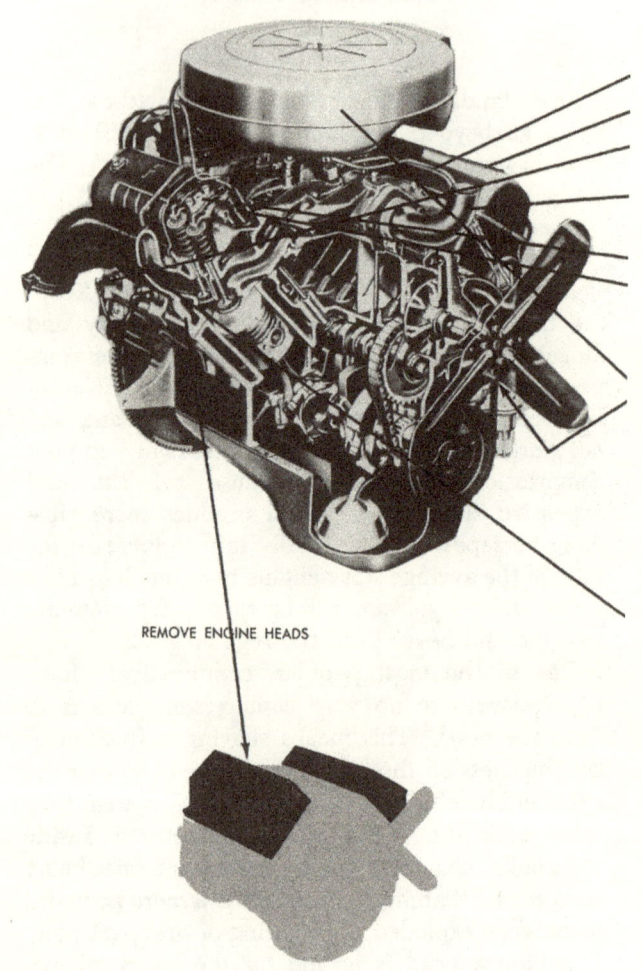

REMOVE ENGINE HEADS

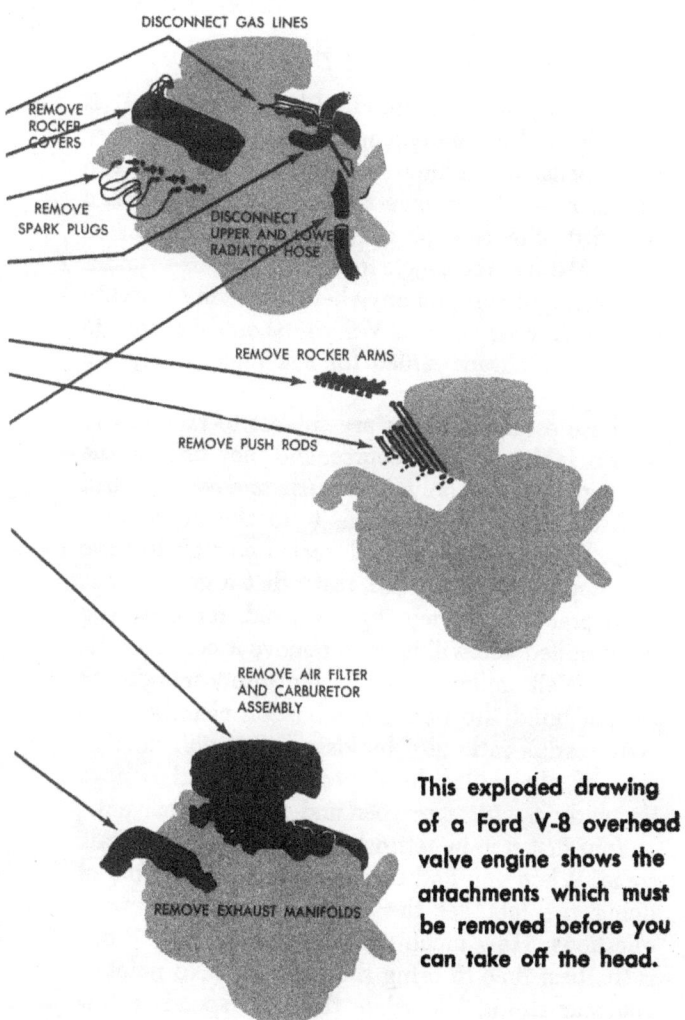

This exploded drawing of a Ford V-8 overhead valve engine shows the attachments which must be removed before you can take off the head.

shaving is just a few hundredths of an inch. It is possible to buy high-compression heads, but they are expensive, running as much as $100. You can get the head of your own engine milled for less than one fifth the cost of a special high-compression head. Milling the single head from a six-cylinder engine might cost you anywhere from ten to twenty dollars. If your car is a V-8 you should be able to get the two heads milled for less than twenty-five dollars.

Those estimated costs are subject to facilities in your neighborhood, of course, and they refer to the milling operation only. You must remove the head yourself, clean it, and take it to the automotive shop. Even if you feel well heeled enough to have the shop do the entire job, resist that urge. You will need practice at removing the head, for after you get it milled you will have to remove it occasionally. Why? Well, milling reduces your safety margin. As carbon builds up in the combustion chambers the compression ratio also builds up. You will have to take off the milled head periodically and remove the carbon with a scraper and a carbon solvent.

Your first step in getting the head milled is to talk some. When you find the machine shop capable of doing the job, get the answers to the following questions: How much will the milling cost? When is the best time to bring the head in? (No point in your car sitting idle while the head spends a few days waiting its turn to be shaved.) Does the shop know the compression ratio of your model, and thus

Backyard Customizing

know how much may be shaved from the head without eliminating the safety margin?

After you have these details straightened out, plan to remove the head in plenty of time to bring it into the shop on the day, or on the hour, on which you have agreed. The illustrations on pages 22 and 23 give you the step-by-step method of removing the head from a stock model car. Although the exact location and design of some engine attachments differ from make to make, these are basically the steps you will follow on any model automobile.

1. Drain the cooling system by opening the petcocks at the bottom of the radiator and on the engine block. If you have antifreeze or Dowguard, or any permanent fluid in your cooling system, you may want to save it.

2. Disconnect the upper and lower hoses at the engine (not at the radiator).

3. Disconnect the ignition wires (necessary on most models, not all) and remove spark plugs. Plugs sometimes get broken if left in the head while dismantling.

4. Disconnect gas line from carburetor.

5. Remove air cleaner if necessary. (Necessary only on a few models.)

(If you are milling an overhead valve V-8 Ford, after you disconnect the hoses from the engine take the rocker covers off the top. Remove the rocker arms, which are held on by long stud screws through the heads. Remove the push rods. Take off the center [intake] manifold; the carburetor and air cleaner assembly come off with it.)

6. Remove the bolts that hold the exhaust manifold to the side of the head (overhead valve engines only). After the head is off, drop the bolts back in place in the manifold for safekeeping.

7. Remove cylinder head bolts. On most models the bolts are studs, and should come off with a reasonable effort. However, a few models have nuts holding the heads in place. The nuts sometimes get frozen and you may have to pry them off, a difficult job at the best.

8. Lift off the head.

During the time the head is at the shop there are other jobs that you can do while the engine is disassembled. A few little chores now will get you the maximum benefit out of the reworked head.

First, if the spark plugs are not ready to be replaced, clean them. Turn each plug upside down and inspect the electrodes for carbon deposits. The electrodes are the two metal points with the little gap between them. Scrape them gingerly with a pocketknife, then sand them with fine sandpaper until both points are bright and clean. Now check the gap. You can get a spark plug gap gauge at any automobile supply store for less than a dollar.

You may have to ask the mechanic who is milling the head to tell you what the correct gap should be. Find the corresponding number (it's in thousandths of an inch) on the feelers in your gap gauge and insert it (or them) between the firing points on the plug. If the feeler moves between the points too freely, hold it in place and firmly squeeze the outer electrode down until the two points have a snug grip on the feeler. If the feeler will not fit in the gap, use a screwdriver to gently but firmly pry the lower point away from the inside electrode.

Next, change your oil filter. When you buy the new one, the auto store selects the correct size for your car. Complete instructions for making the change are printed and illustrated on the box the filter is packed in. Standard filters—the types you throw away when clogged—usually cost between one and two dollars, and sometimes are on sale at less than one dollar. The permanent filters—which you remove and clean when clogged—cost five to ten dollars.

If you know how to tear down a carburetor, now is an ideal time to take it apart and clean it. You need the proper gauge to set the float level when you put the carburetor together again, and you must know exactly how to do it, so don't tackle this job on your own unless you have already learned how it is done. You can, however, clean the air filter that sits on top of the carburetor. This is a job that requires no mechanical skill. Simply remove the wing nut that holds the filter in place, remove the filter, and steep or slosh it in a bucket of kerosene. Set it out to dry before replacing it.

Now, when you get your milled head back, put everything back in place and you have a higher-compressioned, slightly more economical power plant at a total cost of $30.00, more or less. There are other, more advanced alterations which may be peformed on your engine, but the know-how for such jobs must come through experience. Some examples of engine improvements the real dragsters have evolved are:

Porting. When you shave off some metal from the inside wall of the air ports of the cylinders it is called "hogging down the ports" or "porting." Porting allows more air to flow into the cylinder. More air means a bigger explosion and more compression on each stroke of the engine. Not many years ago, any attempt to soup up an engine invariably called for porting. For the past several years, however, automobile manufacturers have been providing a more generous air intake in most models. Practically none of the late-model V-8 engines requires porting by the hot rodder unless he also has his engine bored and stroked. Porting is a tricky and laborious job, too tricky for the amateur. It is expensive to have it done in a shop. (Chapter 4 explains how porting is done.)

Multicarburetion. The job of the carburetor is to shoot the correct amount of gas into the stream of air (after the air has passed through the air cleaner) as it is being sucked into each cylinder. The old-style carburetor—the dual-barrel type still found on many cars—dragged the same amount of air through the filter on each operation. Since the air had to travel different distances to each cylinder, the cylinders farthest from the air cleaner received a richer mixture than did the cylinders directly under the cleaner. The hot-rodding fraternity soon created a market for extra carburetors, and the best all-round solution seemed to be the four-barrel carburetor. Stock-car makers are borrowing the lead from the hot rodders, and the four-barrel carburetor is standard equipment on all V-8's now being built by Detroit. However, if you pick up a stock car that is a few years old you may find yourself altering the carburetor and intake manifold hookup.

Before you make any changes in your carburetor, however, keep in mind that increased carburetion may be too much of a good thing. Some customizers have shortened the lives of their engines by fitting them with four dual-barrel or two four-barrel carburetors. Overcarburetion burns up both fuel and cylinder walls as wantonly as sharp fast turns burn tires. The safest and most economical solution to a lone dual carburetor is to find a factory-built manifold with a four-barrel carburetor that will fit your power plant.

Dual Exhausts. Two chrome tail pipes jutting out of the rear end of a rod are not always strictly for show. The exhaust gas and vapors that result after the explosion in the cylinder must be carried away to make cylinder room for the fresh mixture of air and gas. The stock exhaust system with a standard muffler is adequate for a street vehicle, but if you mill the head or otherwise soup up your engine you may need a more rapid exhaust. Some rodders remove the muffler, since the baffles inside that cut down the noise also cut down the speed with which the exhaust gas moves through. However, antinoise laws in most towns prohibit the elimination of the muffler. The most workable solution is two separate exhaust systems, each with a muffler and each leading from one bank of cylinders.

Beyond altering the head, the carburetor, and the exhaust system, what other gadgets you add to your engine depends upon how gullible you can get. If you are willing to believe you can get several hundred miles per gallon out of your power plant you might become an A-1 customer for the stream of doodads being sold by auto stores and mail-order houses. For instance, here are a few of many "gas and oil savers" selected from just one mail-order catalog:

> *Carburetor adjustment needle with built-in air flow.*
> *Special design carburetors.* (Lots of designs.)
> *Packed mufflers.* (Packing is spun glass or steel.)
> *Crankcase replacement plugs.* (Neutralizes acids.)
> *Magnetic trap for fuel pump.* (Traps metallic particles in gas.)

Choke heater. (Cures plugged passages in choke.)

Humidifying air breather. (Adds moisture to gas and air mixture.)

Dual points. (Eliminates "bucking" at slow speeds, missing at high speeds.)

Freewheeling hub for fan. (Disconnects fan when car goes over a certain speed. The idea is that speed of vehicle sucks in enough air to cool the motor and thus fan does not bleed horsepower from the engine.)

Water-pressure gas injector. (Gives high-octane power to regular gas.)

In theory, and usually in practice, any one of these gimmicks would improve the operation of an automobile engine. Several of them are incorporated into the power plants of racing cars. It is too easy, however, to overrate the added mileage they give to a gallon of gas. Your car would cover several thousand miles before the fuel saving would offset the price of each gimmick.

The Body Job

That road hugging you see on the south end of a northbound rod is a result of one of the most economical methods of changing the silhouette of a stock car. It can be accomplished with a pair of bags of sand placed in the trunk. The sandbags won't put any strain on your vehicle's rear end, provided of course that you avoid overloading with passengers. You can also drop the rear end by attaching U-shaped lowering blocks which may cost as little as four dollars a pair.

Lowering your hot rod at the front axle, rear axle, or both, is a job you will find fairly simple to do yourself. Too simple, for it is done so easily that you can lose sight of the beating your car takes when it is nearer to the ground. Lowering of the body can result in banged bumpers or tail pipe when you take a sharp climb from a level road or level off sharply after coming downhill—and this is a common situation in just getting in and out of some driveways.

Stock kits for lowering are available through several auto parts suppliers. They advertise blocks that will lower the rear end from two to four inches, and the front end from one and a half to two and a half inches.

You can also lower the rear by "Z-ing" the frame. This is a job for the body expert. It involves the cutting of two notches in each frame. One is a V-shaped notch just forward of the wheel, the other an inverted V immediately to the rear of the axle. In both cases the two extremes from where each notch is cut must be brought together and welded. Thus, in closing the two notches, the frame is changed where it curves downward from a gradual curve to a sharp drop, giving you as much as five inches.

There are other methods of Z-ing, some easier and some more difficult than the one just described. Check around among other hot rodders and com-

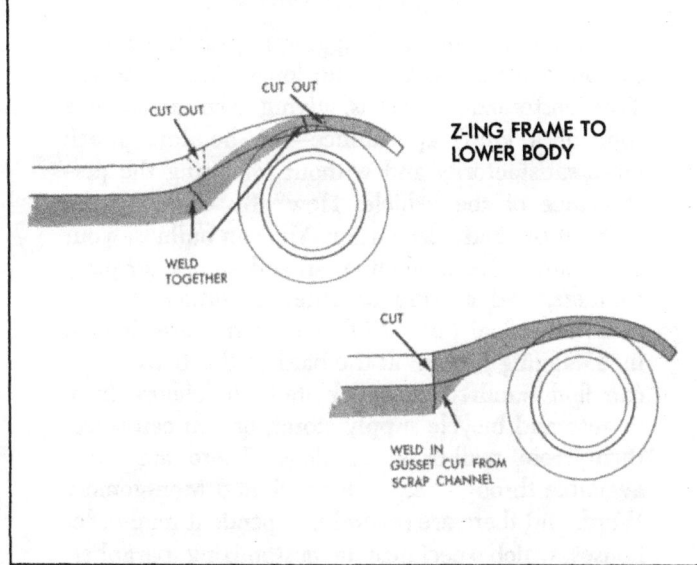

One of several methods of "Z-ing" the frame. Z-ing calls for welding skill, and it may drop the body by as much as five inches.

pare their experiences before you decide on which method of lowering you aim to tackle. Remember, the only advantage is in the silhouette. You may hear talk about the car hugging the road better and cornering more efficiently, but the additional so-called efficiency seldom justifies the bumpy, banging ride you will get on any stretch of rutted road.

So much for the tail-dragging appearance that is so common now as to be no longer "customizing." True customizing—that is, giving your machine a "one of a kind" appearance—can be done much more satisfactorily and without impairing the performance of the vehicle. How? By changing the motif of the body decoration. You can bullnose your car or strip it completely, then add flames, striping, spinners, and a score of other alterations to suit your individual taste. (All these terms are defined in "Dragging Jargon" at the back of this book.) You can find hundreds of stock items to choose from in auto and bicycle supply stores, or you can select them from mail-order catalogs. There are some available through Sears, Roebuck and Montgomery Ward, and there are several independent mail-order houses which specialize in customizing paraphernalia for hot rods.

The customary first step in altering the body appearance is a combination of bullnosing, stripping, and shaving. Bullnosing means the removal of hood ornaments. Stripping means removal of most or all of the chrome, sometimes including the maker's insignia, the door handles, the front grille, and possibly some paint. The holes left after removing the chrome can be filled with fiber glass, covered by a smooth metal strip. Flames—contrasting colors you paint on to cover the area where the chrome was—take away the Detroit look.

Here is a brief rundown on a few of the many items you can add to either the trim or silhouette of your vehicle. These are all nonfunctioning gadgets. You add them purely for appearance. Wherever we have been able to determine the gadget's cost it is given in an approximate price range:

> *Louvers for hood and fenders.* (Approximately 50¢ each. You seldom use less than a dozen.)
>
> *Fender skirts.* (From $8 to $15 a pair. You can get real-gone bubble skirts at $40 a pair.)
>
> *Chrome or gold-finish license-plate holders.* ($1 to $6 each.)
>
> *Continental tire and rear deck.* Adds to the length of your car and carries the spare tire in sporty style. ($50 and up. Mostly up.)
>
> *Front-end grilles.* (Purchased in parts, $10 to about $40.)
>
> *Wheel discs.* ($16 to $50 per set of four.)
>
> *Wheel spinners.* ($1 to $5 each. The less-than-a-dollar types are small, usually requiring three to dress up one wheel.)
>
> *Decals.* (You can spend anything from pennies up, way up, on decals. You can get a metalliclike gold plastic for trim or panel coverage at about $2 per square foot. You can convert your roof to a plaid pattern for $12 to $15. You can get polka dots, gaudy striping, gruesome Dali-type characters, club names, personal names, and so on.)

Other gadgets are available to enhance the silhouette and appearance of your car and are also functional. Some of these are: Fancy lights that resemble tail fins at the rear or rocket cones up front. Dual headlights to give older cars a new-model look. Streamlined rearview mirrors. Chrome extensions for exhaust pipes.

You can also add guards and "bullets" to front and rear bumpers. In short, you will never have enough money to spend on all the trim that is available or have enough car area to hold all the trim. With such limitless variety you can't miss operating a car that is unmistakably yours. Lots of folks will tell you so, with differing inflections in their voices.

Now comes a little cold water. Nothing you add to your car will increase its "book value." If it is wrecked in an accident you will never get back the money you have invested in it, regardless of whether you or the other driver is responsible for the collision. Insurance companies will not pay more than the fair value of the original vehicle before customizing. That fair value is based upon the model and age of the car. That means that any hot rodder who indulges in kid-stuff driving is gambling his valuable property against nothing. That's a mighty poor gamble. Once you have invested money, time, and skinned knuckles in customizing your own hot rod, you will realize how much you can lose by the wrong turn of a wheel.

4. The Real Rail Job

A ROADSTER roaring down a drag strip at 118 miles an hour, a square block of metal where the steering wheel should be, and no driver visible...

A 1934 Ford coupé chopped down so that the roof is barely four inches higher than the hood, the driver sitting practically on the floor with a water tank occupying what should be his passenger's seat...

An elongated silver pencil on four wheels, with the driver perched in the tail, well beyond the rear wheels...

A mechanized skeleton approaching 100 miles an hour as it streaks down the strip, the driver strapped into an oversized motorcycle seat...

Dragging and Driving

An engine, a gas tank, and a set of roll bars surrounding a helmeted driver, all with no visible connection to the four wheels that propel them . . .

These are the rail jobs, the draggin' wagons, the hottest of the hot rods. The most efficient combustion engines ever improvised propel these vehicles, engines for which hundreds of dollars and scores of man-hours have been invested for each small surge of extra power. To the drivers and the race spectators the hot rod is a hobby and a source of thrills. The spectators mostly take their thrills second hand; the drivers and their crewmen enjoy personal exhilaration. To the automobile industry the hot-rodding fraternity represents valuable research—research in perfecting the combustion engine, research in automobile body design, and research in safety gear. Yes, safety. For all the horsepower he crams into the chopped-down, streamlined body, the dragster drives a safe race. The drag strips have not yet been spattered with the blood you find staining Indianapolis and Le Mans.

Whatever the hot rodder does to his engine is of interest to the automotive engineers of Detroit. The many things that the hot rodder adds or shaves off his power plant he adds or shaves to achieve one simple goal. That goal is to get every piston in his engine to deliver the maximum power with every compression stroke. He wants that power to turn his drive wheels with a minimum of energy lost in getting to the wheels. To accomplish this his engine

The Real Rail Job

must suck in the most efficient mixture of fuel and air, force it into the cylinders in correct rotation and in the fastest time possible, then lose no time in getting completely rid of the exhaust gas so that there is full room in the cylinders for the next firing cycle.

The average drag race driver usually starts his hot-rodding career by rebuilding a standard V-8 engine. He will immediately strip it down and go through most, if not all, of the following alterations:

Porting. The purpose of porting, as indicated in the previous chapter, is to make the engine "breathe better"—that is, to get a rapid flow of gas into the cylinders. A high-speed grinder is used to enlarge the inside diameters of the intake and exhaust ports, and to remove any surface bumps inside the ports. Not more than one eighth of an inch may be shaved from the ports or you will risk piercing the engine block and springing a leak in the water jacket.

Further porting is the changing of the angle of the valve seat from the usual forty-five degrees to thirty degrees. This also calls for streamlining the valves and honing down the edges from a normal forty-five to thirty degrees, so that they meet the corresponding thirty-degree angle of the valve seat. This is precision work, and you can see why only experts with appropriate power tools may tackle it.

Relieving. Grinding the engine block between the valves and cylinders is called "relieving the block." The purpose is to widen the passageway for gas

PORTING AND POLISHING

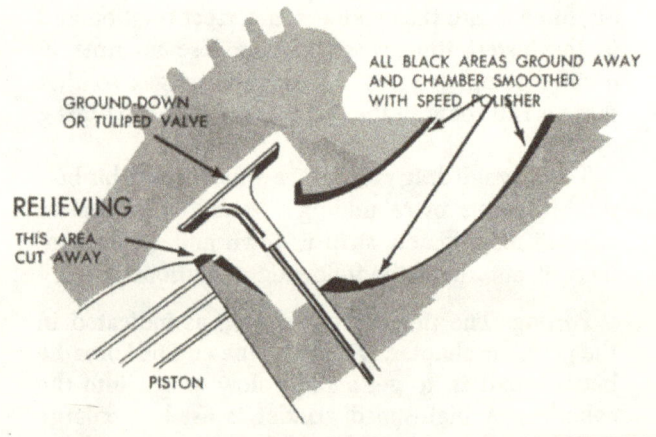

Porting and polishing make the engine "breathe easier." Power tools are used to grind and buff the intake and exhaust ports.

on its travels to the combustion chamber. This, too, is skilled mechanical work and a little overgrinding can result in serious damage to your engine. Relieving should automatically follow the porting of the older flathead engines; it is not necessary when porting the overhead-valve engine.

Polishing. This is a power-tool polishing, not a rag-wiping operation. Ports should be polished after they have been enlarged. Many hot rodders decide to omit porting and just polish the ports and the

BORING

ORIGINAL CYLINDER AND PISTON

REBORED CYLINDER WITH LARGER PISTON

"Boring" is enlarging the diameter of the cylinder. Once you bore the cylinders, you must replace the pistons with a larger set.

combustion chamber. Polishing without porting will still make for a substantial improvement in engine efficiency.

Boring. Perhaps the most efficient way to get more horsepower out of a stock engine is to enlarge the diameter of the cylinder. This is what the

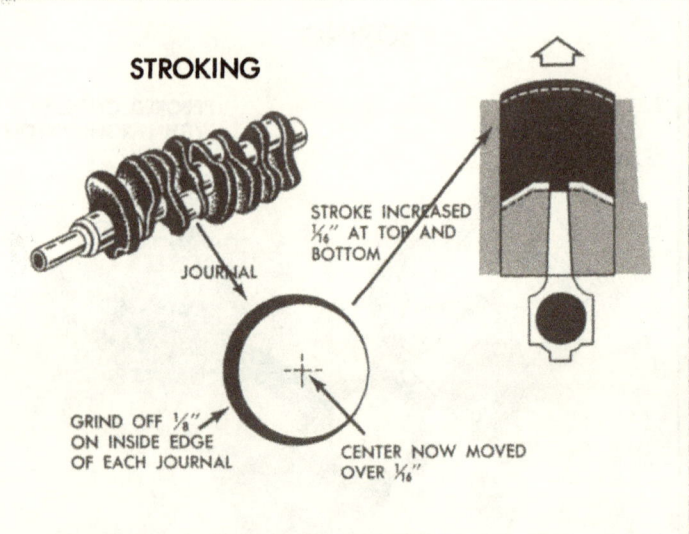

"Stroking" is a method of alerting the camshaft to increase the down stroke of each piston, thus sucking more fuel into each cylinder.

automotive men call "boring." After the cylinders are bored it is necessary to replace the pistons with a larger set and to add a head gasket with a bigger bore.

Stroking. To get still more fuel into the larger combustion chamber (after boring or other alterations) some hot rodders alter the crankshaft. This is "stroking." Instead of shaving, however, metal is welded onto the crank to build it up. Next, the crankpin center is moved a little off the old center so that the piston drops a fraction of an inch lower on the downstroke, thus drawing in more fuel.

Adding carburetion. The carburetor swallows fuel and air and feeds it to six or eight hungry cylinders. Add one more carburetor and the work is cut in half; each cylinder gets its share of fuel faster, though not twice as fast. The competition hot rodder uses a minimum of three carbs. Sometimes he may use eight, one for each cylinder.

Multiple carburetion is strictly for the racing vehicle. When you have three or more carburetors ramming fuel into the cylinders, any attempt at slow traveling means a rough, bone-shaking ride with the engine burning gas like crazy. It is possible, of course, to add carburetors in a hookup that will let you cut out all but one when you are driving at street speeds.

Cleaner cleaners. Each obstruction to the air entering your combustion engine puts that much of a drag on its performance. The air cleaner that sits on top of the stock carburetor is a partial block to incoming air, but on the other hand it screens out dust which would otherwise gum up the valves and pistons. The standard cleaner forces the air to travel through an oil bath. The hot rodder usually changes over to a mesh-type cleaner that filters the large particles of dust but does not restrict the flow of air quite so much as the oil-bath cleaner does. A few dragsters fit their carburetors with "velocity stacks" and resign themselves to sacrificing air cleanliness to get an increase of horsepower. The maximum horsepower increase is about three, so you can see there is little justification for velocity stacks on anything except a competition chariot.

Adding manifolds. Increasing the carburetion provides faster mixing of gas and air for the cylinders, but getting the mixture from the carburetors to the cylinders requires some expansion of the intake manifold operation. The hot rodder has several manifold kits he can choose from. He can also find an adapter that will convert his stock manifold to a dual manifold. Adapters are less expensive than multiple manifolds, but are also less efficient. The adapter will, of course, increase the efficiency of the stock manifold.

Multiple exhausts. When he opens a network of channels that feed more fuel into the cylinders at a faster rate, the hot rodder creates a need to get the exhaust gases out of the cylinders with equally increased speed. Vapors and gases that linger in the exhaust system create a back pressure that robs the next combustion stroke of some power. So the dragster cuts in a set of pipes he calls "headers." Headers provide each cylinder with its own escape channel. The header leads the exhaust out of the engine with a minimum of bends and without the obstructing baffles found inside a muffler.

Headers are the gleaming pipes you see adorning

The Real Rail Job

the sides of a hot rod's engine, three or four on each side. Most headers shoot the exhaust gas down toward the vehicle's rear, although a few gaudy rods have pipes that carry the exhaust up and back. The mouths of some pipes reach to the roof of the vehicle.

There are other refinements—scores of others—all designed to increase the horsepower of stock engines and to deliver that horsepower to the wheels with less waste and more speed. Fuel injectors may be installed to force-feed fuel into each cylinder instead of relying on the stock gravity feed system. Ignition systems are pampered, sometimes souped up to deliver far more than the six or twelve volts the battery provides. Superchargers, using fans or impellers, are used to ram a compressed mixture of fuel and air into the engine. Lightening the weight decreases the drain on horsepower, so various parts of the engine are shaved to save a few ounces or a few pounds (as much as nine pounds can be shaved from the flywheel). The hot rodder often uses alcohol or fuels more combustible than gasoline.

Complicated and laborious as all this customizing seems, it does make sense when the competition rodder alters his engine to get a fraction more power and a few more yards out of each gallon of fuel. He doesn't fool himself or anyone else about "economy." Though he may "save" on fuel he pays the price a hundred times over in the frequent alterations and adjustments to his power plant. He is buying more distance, speed, and power to the gallon and he's convinced it is worth the price.

5. Getting into Competition

SMACK in the middle of our century, the twentieth, Santa Ana, California, was the first community to take an unprejudiced look at hot rodding and then ask itself, "What's wrong with drag racing?"

In the late 1940's that question would easily get you a dozen answers from as many "irate citizens," all unfavorable and all fiery. But after the Santa Ana board of supervisors asked and listened, it was obvious that the beefs boiled down to one solid and legitimate objection—*where*, not *what*. The citizens were understandably worried about dragsters on public roads causing accidents which might kill and maim citizens, including the dragsters.

So Santa Ana provided a drag runway and

coaxed hot rodders to abandon dragging on public roads. That was 1950, but it took some time before other American communities recognized hot rodding as a constructive outlet for the automotive-minded youth of an automotive-minded nation. For one thing, insurance on a drag strip called for high premiums, higher premiums than most communities or taxpayers were willing to pay. The public, as the public is unfortunately inclined to be, was skeptical of encouraging automobile speed contests. Here and there one venturesome organization or some citizens got together and a few legitimate drag strips began to replace "race-and-git-before-the-cops-come" dragging on public highways. Finally, the National Hot Rod Association broke the financial opposition with an insurance package at a bargain price. Now hot rodding roared into the realms of legality and respectability like a bent eight bomb.

One result is that the drag race is now fair competition, with races being run under rules and over measured courses. The course is one quarter mile. You get 1,320 feet in which to wheedle the maximum acceleration out of your vehicle. You cross the finish line and either you are first or you are not. This is the sanctioned strip's major advantage over street drags. On the strip you don't hear a sorehead screeching his rubber past you a mile beyond the finish line as though he had just been giving you a handicap back there where you beat his time.

There are now nine major divisions of rods in

which a dragster can compete at most organized drag races. There are also annual national championships for all nine divisions, with different classes within each division, based upon weight, size and some assorted etceteras. Here are the official NHRA classifications:

G for gas coupé and sedan. Cars in this division are stock models with souped-up engines. Each car must be fully equipped with the essentials of legal on-the-street driving. G is divided into five classes by weight and engine displacement (specified in cubic inches).

SR for street roadster. Cars in this division are American production roadsters and open pickup bodies. The SR rod, like the G division, must be equipped for legal driving on public roads and essentially used for normal transportation. There are two SR classes, based upon weight and engine displacement.

A for altered coupé and sedan. Cars in this division may have undergone moderate alterations from the stock vehicles. The engine may be relocated, but under certain limitations. Fenders may be removed or not. There are three classes in the A division.

R for roadster. This division is for American production roadsters or open pickups. Fenders are optional, and a limited relocation of the engine is permitted. There are two classes in the R division.

Getting into Competition 49

C for competition coupé and sedan. (Now we're getting closer to the bomb.) C cars may be radically modified and streamlined. Engines may be moved back quite a piece. However, the C division vehicle must have originated as a production car. Two C classes are raced.

M for modified roadster. Here again is what was originally an American production car. It may not be recognizable, however, for radical alterations in body and engine are permitted. There are two M classes.

D for dragster. This is the unique machine which drag racing itself has spawned. The dragster is assembled for one single purpose—to travel one quarter mile in the shortest time within its potential, then to do it in less time on the next run. The only limitations are NHRA compulsory safety requirements. There are three competition classes for the dragster.

X for four barrel. This is the division that keeps the four-cylinder production cars alive long past their original prime. Some X cars were assembled by auto manufacturers who went out of business before your father ever heard of them, but surviving vehicles are still zooming down the drag strips. There is only one X class.

Sp for sports car. The baby of drag racing, sports cars entered NHRA national competition in 1956. The Sp must carry full equipment for legal street driving, and the engine must remain in its original location. Sp cars run in five classes, based upon engine displacement.

Any drag racing you are likely to do will probably start with the G or SR divisions. Both of these possibilities are within your reach, especially if you join up with a hot-rod club. If you don't know where the club nearest to you can be found, write and ask the National Hot Rod Association, 1171 N. Vermont Avenue, Los Angeles 29, California.

It there is no club near you, start your own. The easiest way is to get a "sponsor" for your club. Sponsors can be found anywhere. Ask the state or municipal police, your local safety council, chamber of commerce, your church officials, an automobile dealer, auto supply store (especially if it's a speed shop), perhaps even school officials.

You are going to get some opposition from adults, including some of the organizations suggested above as sponsors. Some police departments sponsor hot-rod clubs or drag strips, while other police departments are dead against both. One reason you find police not in favor of drag strips is that in some towns where strips are provided, some hot rodders still barrel down public roads and cause accidents. When picked up they often turn out to be drag strip regulars. One squirrel can louse up the deal for everybody.

The National Hot Rod Association may be a source of help if you run into local opposition. Write to the association at the address given above. The NHRA can also suggest many activities for your hot-rod club. Most of these activities have a double purpose. First, they provide fun. Second, they get you in good with adult citizens. They bring out some solid citizens who act friendly toward teen-agers with cars.

Low Saddle Roadeo

There's a new type roadeo, podnuh, in which you can ride 145 horses or more, without straining yourself to stay on the comfortable foam-rubber saddle. It's the Teen-Age Road-e-o, and it will draw over a half-million contestants this year or any year. Every state in the Union will find a state champion to send to Washington, D.C., for the finals. The top three finalists of the National Teen-Age Road-e-o win college scholarships of $2,000, $1,500, and $1,000.

You compete in the Road-e-o by the skill in which you handle a stock car over a special course. Pennants and metal barrels are used to mark out some tight situations, most of them patterned after the famous course of the truck drivers' annual roadeo.

The teen-agers' version of the roadeo is run by the United States Junior Chamber of Commerce, popularly known as the "Jaycees." The Jaycees handle the competition, backed by such sponsors as Chrysler Corp., Liberty Mutual Insurance Company, the American Trucking Associations, Inc., and the Pure Oil Company.

All you need to qualify for the Teen-Age

Road-e-o is a driver's license. You have to be a teenager, of course, and that means if you are not older than nineteen, up to and including August 15 of the year, you may enter that year's contest. You may have to provide your own car for the local contest, but if you make the national championships the sponsors provide the cars. Two things you cannot have if you want to be eligible for the Road-e-o: One is a moving traffic violation within the six months preceding August 1, and the other is a job as a driver of a commercial vehicle.

To compete in the Teen-Age Road-e-o, look up your nearest local Junior Chamber of Commerce (Jaycee) and ask for information or an entry blank. You can find the Jaycee office through the telephone book, your local newspaper office, or the (senior) Chamber of Commerce office. If you can find no Jaycee organization nearby, write to:

Teen-Age Road-e-o Committee
U. S. Junior Chamber of Commerce
Jaycee Boulevard and Main Street
Tulsa, Oklahoma

6. So You're Stuck with the Stock

MAYBE it's not so much that you are stuck with a stock-model car that for various reasons you cannot customize. Perhaps it is just that you've come to the conclusion that the world's number one automotive nation reached that position because it has the best mechanical brains and the best automotive designers to produce their multi-billion-dollar product, the American automobile.

On the other hand, perhaps the car you drive is not your exclusive property. Even in a two-car family you will often find three or more members holding drivers' licenses. In that case, if each driver had a free hand in adorning the car you might wind up with a vehicle that looked as though it housed a circus calliope.

There is fun and satisfaction in keeping an automobile looking as sleek and running as smoothly as the day it rolled out of the showroom. The leveling off of new-car sales in the past few years is one indication that many families have realized that they are going to have to squeeze another ten or twenty thousand miles out of the vehicle they bought a few years ago. You can help add a few thousand miles to the life of your car and do it while utilizing some of the techniques the hot rodder uses to build faster acceleration into his hack. The basic techniques are the same, but you don't go all out and you don't use the same expensive equipment. You can keep the family stock in purring condition without altering the engine, and save the family treasury a small sum on gasoline expenditures and possibly a large sum on engine maintenance and repairs.

To service a car does not require years of training or garage experience. Mostly it calls for knowing the principle of how the engine works, and that principle is relatively simple in spite of all the bulges and bowls attached to the engine block. The engine sucks in a vast amount of air, mixes the oxygen (only 21 per cent of the air is oxygen) with a little gasoline, then ignites the mixture to create an explosive force which drives the crankshaft. The crankshaft may be likened to an assembly that pedals the rear wheels. Your foot pushes bicycle pedals, but the compression stroke of the engine cylinder pedals the automobile.

So You're Stuck with the Stock

All the bulges and bowls attached to the engine function to make this cycle happen as smoothly as possible and to get rid of the used exhaust gases as well as the unused 79 per cent of the air. By keeping those attachments in the best working condition you can give your engine considerable help toward functioning economically and requiring a minimum of repair work.

First, and something which the average driver is inclined to forget, is to ride herd on the plugs. Spark plugs should be clean and gapped properly. Theoretically, you should remove the plugs every 2,500 miles, wipe them clean, and inspect them for carbon deposits. During long spells of damp weather, plug inspections should be more frequent. It is also good medicine to check the plugs at shorter mileage intervals if the car is more than five years old or has more than 50,000 miles on the odometer. A balky engine sometimes is a sign that plugs need changing or cleaning. Balkiness shows up in several symptoms: engine bucking or laboring when climbing an incline; odor of gasoline inside the car; noticeable drop in the mileage you get out of each gallon.

When you remove a spark plug you can usually tell at a glance whether it is helping or hurting the engine. If the plug is still in good shape it will be coated lightly with dry soot or flaky carbon at the base. The electrodes may have eroded a little at the spark point, but otherwise should be intact. The porcelain will be light brown or gray and may also have a light coating of powder.

If the porcelain is blistered or cracked, and the base coated with a chalky-white deposit, the plug is too hot for your model engine. If it is coated with heavy, oily deposits or carbon or soot at the base, the plug is too cold. In either case, get new plugs. Buy the resistor-type spark plug that is recommended for your model car—either by the makers of your car or the manufacturer of the spark plug. Before installing new plugs be sure that the gap is correct.

You can do a fair job of cleaning spark plugs with a pocketknife and fine sandpaper. You can do an excellent job if you have access to the sandblast type of cleaner found in some service stations. If the plugs are rusty or already have been cleaned a few times, it is wiser economy to throw them away and buy a new set. After each cleaning check the gap between the electrodes with a gap gauge. If you still have the owner's manual which came with the car when it was new, look under "ignition" or "electrical system" to find the proper gap. If the manual has long since gone, remember to ask the clerk at the store where you buy the new plugs. He has a chart and can look up the gap recommended for your engine.

Next, look at your oil filter. Many drivers will pay for a complete change of oil at the beginning of each season and never think to change the filter. Gunk can build up in the filter to the point where oil is forced to channel its way through without being filtered. In a short time a clogged filter can nullify your complete oil change.

On the other hand (some oil refiners and service station operators will shudder at this) by continually monitoring your filter you may never need to change your oil. If you keep the filter clean you are effecting a change of oil by simply replacing depleted oil with new oil of the right viscosity for the season of the year. The ideal way to keep your filter clean is to buy the permanent type and dunk it frequently in kerosene or gasoline.

Other parts of the engine need periodic cleaning or lubrication. Some you can service yourself; others you may need to have done at a service station. Either way, it will help you if you have the recommendations of the manufacturer of your car. In general, you will find that the average car will be more dependable if you follow this schedule.

Every 1,000 Miles or 30 Days

Remove carburetor air cleaner and clean it in kerosene. If it has a reservoir, empty that out and refill to proper level with engine oil. Use S.A.E. 50 for summer driving, S.A.E. 30 for winter driving.

If there is a lubricant fitting on the water pump, add water-pump grease.

Lubricate linkage for hand brake and gearshift with engine oil.

Lubricate pedal linkage and bell crank with chassis lubricant.

Every 2,500 to 3,000 Miles

Clean or replace spark plugs.

Clean permanent oil filter. (If filter is the standard nonpermanent type, replace it every 10,000 miles, sooner if necessary. Inspect it whenever changing plugs.)

Check oil level in engine (if it is not done periodically by service station attendant when you buy gas).

Every 10,000 Miles or Every Year

If there are oil cups on your generator (there are usually two) drop about six drops of light engine oil in each. Be stingy. Too much oil can ruin a generator. Be sure to close the covers of the oil cups immediately to keep dirt particles from dropping in.

There is usually one oil cup on the distributor. Drop about six drops of light engine oil in it. Remove the cap and rotor and place two drops of oil on the felt wick on top of the cam. Be careful not to let oil spatter on or near the breaker points.

Replace oil filter (if not done at shorter intervals).

Check lubricant level in the transmission. If it is low, be sure you find the right grade of lubricant to add. On standard transmissions, S.A.E. 10-W is generally recommended. The different types of automatic transmissions, however, call for different lubricants.

Every 20,000 Miles or Every Two Years

Disassemble universal joint and clean and repack it with heavy joint grease. Disassemble shaft spline and clean and repack it half full with chassis lubricant.

Every Spring

Drain antifreeze out of radiator. (You can save the mixture for next winter, but you may have to add a rust inhibitor. Permanent-type antifreeze can lose its qualities for resisting rust.) Flush radiator, then refill it and check all connections for leaks. After you are satisfied there are no leaks, drain off a little water and add a rust inhibitor.

Check muffler. If it is holing out at the bottom, better have it replaced. Tighten all bolts on engine mount and around the body.

Every Winter

Drain radiator, flush, and drain again. Pour in about one gallon of water, add antifreeze, then complete filling with water. If you are using the temporary type of antifreeze you may have to add rust inhibitor. (You can tell by reading the contents printed on your antifreeze container.)

Test defroster and heater.

If you're in snow country, put bag of sand, shovel, and tire chains into the trunk.

Every Season

Check battery, generator, and regulator.
Check headlights, turn signals, tail and stop lights.

Remove trash from grill and radiator core—bugs, leaves, papers, etc.

Get down where you can inspect bottom of doors and body panels. If there are clogged drain holes, clean them with an awl, ice pick, or length of wire coat hanger.

Operate doors and windows, listening closely to each for squeaks. Lubricate with graphite.

Check your clutch foot to see whether the lazy dog is "riding the clutch." You shorten the life of the clutch when you drive with one foot resting on the pedal. "Slipping the clutch" is another habit that makes more business for the repair shop. "Slipping" means using the clutch to hold the car when temporarily stopped on an incline by just pressing the pedal enough to make the clutch do the brake's job.

Every Now and Then

Dry-clean and launder.

The dry cleaning is mostly for the interior. Use the small attachments for the vacuum, some clean dustcloths, hand broom, and, if necessary, chrome polish.

What you use to wash the body may depend upon the finish. (For instance, on a porcelainized body you are advised not to use soap or detergent. After some types of repaint jobs a car cannot be washed for several weeks.) In most cases it is safe to wash with a mild detergent, working a small area, then rinsing it immediately.

So You're Stuck with the Stock

Before wetting the car inspect the lower body areas and the rear bumper deck for tar and oil spots. They can be removed with a rag dipped in kerosene, spot remover, or even lighter fluid. After you use these solvents wipe them off immediately and flush with clean water.

Have the car in the shade, and don't start work until the hood is the same temperature as the rest of the car. In other words, do not wash the hood shortly after the engine has been running for more than ten minutes.

Start by rinsing or hosing the entire car. Wash the glass areas, inside and out. Next wash the four wheels, then the rest of the body from the bottom up. Wash one area, then rinse it before you go to the next area. After you complete the car, give it one more complete rinse or hosing. Wipe dry with chamois or soft rags as free from lint as possible.

More Car Care

Your automobile has many moving parts not located under the hood. These parts, too, will pay you back in service what you give them in attention.

Tires. If your five tires are all in the same general condition, you will get more mileage out of them by rotating them every 2,500 miles or so. It can be done with a single jack if you start by placing the spare on the rear right wheel, then transfer the rest as follows: rear right to front left, front left to rear left, rear left to front right, and front right to spare. If your original spare is not good enough for general wear, you can then remove it again from the rear right wheel, replacing it with the tire which just came off the front right wheel.

Keeping the right inflation in your tires not only helps to lengthen their wearing period, but gives you better road control of your car. The best time to check tire pressure is after the car has traveled for a few hours. Riding builds up pressure inside the tire as much as three to five pounds, depending upon the distance you travel and your average driving speed.

Gas (or accelerator) pedal. Normally the only affliction peculiar to the gas pedal is "heavy foot." Occasionally, however, the pedal may stick when depressed. Should that happen when you must make a quick stop it can be dangerous. A now-and-then preventive measure is to drop a little oil or graphite on the rod under the pedal at the point where it enters the floorboard. If the pedal sticks in spite of lubricating at the floorboard, you may have to get under the hood and oil the linkage.

Windshield wipers. The blades of your windshield wipers tend to pick up grit. When they do they are streaky when operating, especially when other cars splatter your windshield with mud. Every now and then hold the blade away from the windshield and gently draw fine sandpaper along both sides of the edge of the blade. This operation is more successful if performed in dry weather.

Noises. No matter how tightly a car is put together, sooner or later there will be a few squeaks and rattles creeping into an otherwise quiet ride. This is inevitable, since the irregular motions of sudden braking, turning sharp corners, and slamming doors will loosen the hardware. When a new noise develops, every occupant of the car will "hear" it coming from a different location.

Many squeaks and leaks can be prevented if you comb the interior of the car periodically, tightening every visible fastening. Start inside at the driver's position and tighten every screw in the steering wheel assembly; then do the rest of the dashboard. Next, work on the windshield trim, then all door panels. After that, inspect door posts, ceiling, and all other interior hardware for screws or bolts. Draw them tight, but don't bear down after they feel tight. You will wind up listening to a real squeaker if you strip or snap a screw.

Now get outside the car and work your way around from one of the headlights. Check not only the lights, but the rearview mirror bracket, door handles, locks, and chrome strip. If a section of chrome is loose, you may have to pry the whole strip off, then tighten the brackets underneath before you replace it.

Upholstery never gets noisy but does wear more in some spots than in others. Slip covers may protect seats, but armrests and door panels invariably will discolor or break through where they have been rubbed continuously. Auto supply stores sell little plastic covers for armrests. You simply fit them over the armrest, pull a zipper, and that is that. Door panel upholstery can be patched with a preglued fabric similar to patches you find on dungarees. You can buy them in department and dry goods stores and the many varieties of "five and tens." If you need heat to apply the patch you can bring your mother's iron out on a long extension cord. Be careful that you do not scorch the area around the patch.

There are advantages to keeping a car running and looking its best. One advantage to keeping your finger always on the pulse of the engine and not letting it get sick unnecessarily is that the vehicle will be less likely to get balky when you need it. Another advantage to taking the responsibility for keeping the family car looking well and functioning efficiently is that the legal owner is less likely to get balky when you need the car.

Oh yes, there is one other important moving part on the vehicle. It is located toward the rear, built into one fender on some cars, part of the rear deck on others. It is circular and operates easily when you turn it counterclockwise. You can recognize it easily; it looks exactly like the cap to a gas tank. Removing it and filling the tank when required, especially *after* using the car, **is** one more method of keeping both the car and the legal owner happier with your driving.

7. How to be Chicken and Popular

POUND FOR POUND, the chicken has as much guts as any two-legged creature. About the dumbest thing the feathered variety of chicken ever does is to let some slick operator attach a pair of murderous blades to his feet and toss him into a pit to fight some other chicken. Even the winner comes out of the pit looking as though he took a header through a windshield. The one person most indifferent to the fighting cock being clobbered is the human character who conned him into the senseless match.

All of which proves nothing except that the expression "chicken" is meaningless and at the same time contradictory.

I found three drivers with real guts—a trucker

who pilots a big trailer rig, a dragster who coaxed his rod up to 140 miles per hour in eleven seconds, and a turnpike cop who can overtake a speeding car doing ninety-nine miles per hour. I asked each to sound off on driving and drivers.

"Me, I'm chicken," said the truck driver. "I'm a *live* chicken." An unlighted cigarette dangled from his mouth, so I offered to reach over and hold the wheel while he lit up. He never gave me so much as a sidewise glance, but you could feel the atmosphere in the cab stiffening with his back. When he started to talk I expected a chewing out, but instead he asked what seemed like a change-of-subject question.

"Did you ever play drop the dollar?"

"Never heard of it."

A few silent minutes later we pulled over for a coffee stop. Before opening the door on his side he flexed the fingers of both hands and said, "When I let go of that steering wheel you can bet your last dime the other four wheels aren't turning either." *Then* he lit the cigarette and I figured it was just about time for me to hop out.

As soon as he stepped down from the cab he caught me by the arm and pulled a dollar bill out of his pocket. He held the dollar gently by one narrow edge, dangling it down lengthwise.

"Now," he said, "hold your thumb and forefinger about the middle of the buck but keep your fingers about an inch away from it. Don't touch the dollar, but be ready to grab it when you see me let go—

How to be Chicken and Popular

which I'm going to do without giving you warning."

This, I told myself, will be a snap. All I have to do is bring my thumb and forefinger together as soon as he releases his grip and I've got it. After I picked the dollar bill off the ground for the fifth straight time I conceded I wasn't nearly as fast as I had believed.

"Don't feel so bad," he said. "Nobody reacts fast enough to grab the buck. Now and then some guy anticipates the drop at the right split second, and he looks good. But he can't do it the second time. Usually, he gets caught making his grab before you let the bill drop.

"That buck is gone in less than three quarters of a second after you let it go—and three quarters of a second is the fastest reaction time on record. If you could react that fast, and if you were driving down the road at a slow thirty miles per hour, and if a kid ran out into the road thirty-three feet in front of your car, you would hit that kid about the same time your foot hit the brake."

"Doing only thirty?" I asked incredulously.

"Yup. Doing only thirty you travel thirty-three feet in the three quarters of a second it takes for the fastest reaction. You know what happens in that reaction time? You gotta focus your eyes on what's happening, then the eyes send a signal to the brain. The brain's gotta send word to your brake foot. You do that in three quarters of a second and you're fast. Most drivers can't, but they'll never admit they can't."

But thirty-three feet wasn't even the length of his trailer. It seemed to me that if you could stop within that distance you would have pretty good control of your vehicle.

"Who," he demanded, "ever said you could *stop* in thirty-three feet? That's how far you roll before you *start* to *stop*, before your foot is on the brake pedal. At thirty miles per hour on a good road and with good brakes you might be able to bring a passenger car to a stop in another forty-six feet. That means you've traveled seventy-nine feet after you saw what it was that made you try to stop. At forty miles per hour it takes 126 feet. At fifty you cover 186 feet. Want me to go on? Anyway, at eighty miles per hour you will travel farther than Mickey Mantle's ball did when he hit his record home run."

This was the spiel I was getting from a driver who was taking the maximum speed permitted on any highway we traveled. Fifty on state highways, sixty and more on the turnpikes. How come, I wanted to know, he didn't quit driving a truck or have more accidents.

"I don't believe I could answer either of those questions," he said. "But I can sure tell you this: I don't just sit behind this wheel and hope nothing will happen. I defend myself as well as I know how. I'm not mad at anybody on the road, but I figure the best way to keep from getting knocked into next Tuesday is to be something like a prize fighter —keep your defense up, practice fast footwork, always watch the other guy in the ring, and roll with each punch.

"Like now; see how traffic is thickening up on us?" We had finished our coffee (without the "and" —"Too much food makes you a drowsy driver," he said) and we were back on the state highway. The signs indicated we were nearing a town and traffic was building up. "I can see five or six cars ahead because in this cab we are up a little higher than auto drivers. But even in a sedan you can generally see two or three cars ahead. It's a wonder my eyeballs don't get pooped. I'm watching those cars way up front, I'm watching for the next traffic light; I'm looking at both sides of that road that intersects our highway up ahead, and I got my eyes peeled for weavers. When I see the third or fourth car up front put on his brakes I can get my foot on my brake pedal before this joker in front of me can reach his.

"Our outfit hired a high-priced safety engineer, and he told us this is 'watching the big picture.' He says that watching everything not only pays off in itself, but just looking all over the lot like that helps prevent you from getting sleepy. In other words, my eyeballs actually stay more wakeful rather than getting pooped.

"Another thing, I gotta use these two mirrors pretty steady. Look, right now I've got a joker tailgating me. Makes me feel like a wrestler who let his opponent sneak around behind him. Some drivers deliberately slow down to discourage a bumper jockey from riding his tail. That's bad. Me, I flick on my lights. All he sees is the red taillight and he thinks I'm braking. See, our buddy boy has slowed down already and dropped back a few yards. Usually most drivers will stay back. They're not stinkers, just a little absent-minded at times. That's not good either."

Town was the end of the line for us. The trucker dropped his rig at the terminal and we made our way home by train. As one of the year's champions of the National Truck Roadeo he gets an extra $50 per month. He rates it.

In a beat-up shed off Turkey Swamp Road we found a gleaming rod and a beaming teen-ager. Both, in partnership, had recently barreled down a Florida strip at 140 miles per hour.

"You wouldn't catch me doing seventy on any public highway," said dragster Tony Warmsutt, "not even on a turnpike."

Why, you might ask him, would he spook at doing seventy when he had just proved he can handle a car at twice that speed?

"Man," answers Tony, "I'm not afraid of what *my* heap will do. But on a drag strip I know what's on the road all the way down to the finish line. I know there aren't any drivers coming at me who might be on the verge of a heart attack or maybe ready to pass out after one too many for the road. I know the strip gives me a straight road to myself all the way.

"Put it this way," Tony continued, "I'm a good

swimmer and I get a bang out of the high board. But, Pops, you don't catch me diving off the rooftop into a rain puddle. So why should I stake my bomb and my profile against nothing but a phony thrill on a gamble that there won't be some squirrel bombing across the next intersection? That would sure be kookie."

Somehow Tony Warmsutt had put together the time, the money, and the automotive skill to produce a competition vehicle valued at $8,000. Few guys can come up with that combination. Time anybody can find, but money and technique are scarce commodities. This I pointed out to Tony, asking what other guys might look forward to in the way of competition or any other driving thrill. Legal type, that is.

"Gang up," he said.

"How's that again?"

"Gang up. You don't think my own lily-white fingers shaped this draggin' wagon by themselves. We've got a club. The Asphalt Knights. Four of the guys have rods, but the others don't. Hank, here, is saving to get his own rod when he's old enough for a license. He *thinks* I'm lucky. I *know* he's lucky. We'll make most of the goofs in the book on my rod, but by the time the Knights are ready to customize Hank's stock we'll be tops.

"Want to know another thing?" continued Tony. "If you haven't got your own rod you can still compete, as long as you rate the key to the family stock. You don't even have to customize it. Down in

Florida I met some guys who had made last year's finals in the Teen-Age Road-e-o. They run the same type of course as the truck drivers do in their roadeo, except the teen-agers drive stock cars. By making the finals these guys got a free trip to Washington and did they ever have a ball! They never had and didn't need hot rods. Back home they practiced the course in their old men's cars. They got the keys without any beefs, too. Once they copped top money in the locals they didn't even need the family buggy anymore. The Road-e-o people supplied stock jobs to all the finalists—just for the competition, of course, not to keep. Yep, they sure had a ball. Had lots of Hollywood starlets there, too."

"And the vice-president," chimed in Hank.

"Hank's only fourteen," explained Tony.

You couldn't exactly say the trooper was happy to talk about tickets, but he wasn't reluctant. He had just come off a tour of duty on the New Jersey Turnpike.

"I wrote out my first ticket the first day on the job," he said, "and it was for a kid on the same day he got his license. I guess he's forgotten it by now. I haven't. He could have gotten away with a minor violation that day, considering it was a first for both of us, but I'm a real stinker to any driver who deliberately cuts off somebody just for the fun of it."

He couldn't say whether that particular stunt is

pulled more by young drivers or by mature drivers.

"Kid stuff," he snapped, "no matter what age the birth certificate gives. Some guys are still kids when they're over forty—at least as far as their driving goes. Most of these teen-agers are good drivers. You just get to wishing they didn't know that themselves. One of their worst troubles is that they don't allow for the other driver. They figure he's just gonna let 'em barrel through. I'll tell you one thing, though. I'd sooner take my chances on a road crowded with teen drivers than on a road with one drunk. That's another thing I'm a stinker about. When I catch a driver with a snootful, he isn't driving that car another yard. There's a lot of people and cars still on the roads today because cops have pulled drunk drivers right off the highways.

"I'm a romance buster-upper, too," the trooper went on, with a wry smile. " 'Cepting I don't ticket the driver unless he already has a few violations against him. Necking while driving is almost as suicidal as driving drunk or playing wrinkle fender. The only difference is the attitude. I sure hate to lecture anybody, but when I stop a car with a one-arm driver I usually ignore the driver, other than to check his license. Then I tell the chick what a mess a windshield can make out of her pretty face.

"Does it work? I dunno. When you pick up the paper and read about more kids getting ground up into hamburger you wonder if anything works."

Truck driver, dragster, and turnpike patrolman—

three drivers, each with a serious purpose when they get behind a steering wheel. The truck driver's purpose is to make a living and stay alive to enjoy it. The dragster's is to set a record and to live for the next meet to beat his own record. The cop's is to keep other drivers alive in spite of themselves.

Large truck fleet operators are now giving their drivers training in a special five-step formula that is designed to help them avoid accidents—and to stay out of somebody else's accident. The same formula might add years to the life of any vehicle, and any driver.

Correcting your steering habits is the first step. You start out with the handicap of sitting to the left of center in the car, and the average driver cannot gauge the amount of clearance to the right of his vehicle. As a result, even though he is closer to the left side of his vehicle, he will ride in the extreme left portion of his lane, sometimes fudging over the oncoming traffic lane. When an object looms up on the right he gives it much more clearance than it needs. That invites a sideswipe or head-on collision with traffic coming from the other direction.

You can correct lopsided steering by making more use of your "fringe vision." When you drive you have two areas of vision. One area is your center eyesight—a narrow cone of sharp, clear vision. The other area is your fringe vision—a broad but not very clear visual sweep of a large area outside the center eyesight. Fringe vision does not focus sharply on any object, but is quick to spot anything that contrasts with the background—lights or movement, for instance. When your fringe vision does detect something it usually pulls your center eyesight onto it. If you consciously use your fringe vision to watch the center of your lane about 200 feet in front of your car it can keep you traveling straight in the center of the lane. Don't try to keep your center eyesight on the lane. If you stare at the same object for as much as two seconds, chances are your stare becomes blank and your mind fails to "see" any object your eyes are aiming at.

Knowing what's up ahead is the second step. This is the technique the truck driver referred to when he cited the safety engineer's advice about "watching the big picture." Don't keep your eyes fixed rigidly on just the car immediately ahead or on any other single object. Try to sight the cars beyond the one just in front of you. Glance into oncoming traffic. Look for pedestrians, especially small children. Watch for ruts or obstructions farther along the road, so you won't be taken by surprise when a less observant driver must swerve suddenly. Keeping your roving eye on the big picture this way warns you in advance that the driver you are following may have to stop short. It helps you avoid sudden stops yourself, and if nothing else, it saves you money on gasoline and tires.

Developing an all-seeing eye is the third step. Force your eyes to move at least every two seconds. The more you move your eyes, the more you are resting them. Fixed staring is tiresome to eyes, movement is restful. Check your traffic in the rearview mirror often. Check the dials on your dash. At night, be sure you do not allow your eyes to stare at the spot where your headlights sweep the road or you will be hypnotized into a deep sleep. On a long drive, stop occasionally and give your eyes a ten-minute rest.

Avoiding getting booby-trapped is the fourth step. Every driver pulls a road boner now and then. One too common mistake is to shoot suddenly into another lane without first scanning the lane and finding it clear. Never get yourself in a spot where you get rammed because someone else goofed. Always have an exit handy. Maintain a space-cushion distance from the car in front. If he is too slow you will find it easier to pass him from a position thirty feet behind than from ten feet behind. Why? Because you can see the road ahead and can choose the best moment for passing. When you do start to pass, beep two shorts on your horn so he will be less likely to start drifting into your lane just as you come abreast of his car. If it is night, flick your bright lights.

Not being secretive is the fifth step. Let the other wheelman know you are there, and especially let him know when you are about to turn, stop, pass, or slow down. Use your signal devices whenever you turn; make that a habit regardless of whether yours is the only car on the road. In that way signaling will become an automatic part of your driving and you are less likely to forget to signal when forgetting can cause trouble. If your vehicle does not have electric signals, use clear, universal hand signals—you probably had to learn those signals to pass your driver's test.

Don't sneak up on the other driver's blind spot. This is a mistake you can make without much effort when you come up behind a large truck. Make sure you've been visible in his mirror for a minute or two before you signal that you are going to pass him. Once you start to pass trucks or slow cars on a four-lane highway, don't play leapfrog. Stay in the left lane until you have passed all those in the one cluster. Then move over to the right lane and let faster drivers get past you.

Five simple steps, and the experts say that it takes less than two months of practice for any good driver to convert them into habits, the type of habits that make for longevity for cars and drivers.

8. Skids, Skins, and Skills

RACE DRIVERS figure that one way to win a race is to live long enough to finish first. That fact stands in spite of the dramatic news pictures you may have seen of spectacular crack-ups on the race track. The reason why you do see so many newsreel and newspaper shots of racing smashups is that cameras, many of them, are trained on the track for the full duration of the race. If you aimed a battery of cameras on a stretch of U.S. 1 for the same length of time you would photograph a rash of fender bending there, too.

The racing driver with a big share of wins never pushes his car beyond what he knows it can do. The winningest drivers have few accidents on the race

Skids, Skins, and Skills

track and usually none—repeat, none—on the highways.

Because of the nature of his business, the racing driver knows there is always the possibility of a sudden hazard on the track and on the highway. He continually expects the unexpected. He looks for the car in the right lane to suddenly swerve in front of him. When a tire blows he already has two hands ready on the steering wheel; he is never caught with his left hand caressing the roof or door of his buggy. When the race car in front of him skids and ends up crossing his T on the track (the same situation as a car shooting out of a crossroad onto the highway in front of him), he usually knows when and in which direction to swerve; he never panics or cuts right in front of the skidding car.

Skids, skins, and skill. The racing driver knows how to come out of the skid, even when his car is turned completely around and is in a reverse skid. He drives on tires with good treads, but he knows good tires can be as useless as slim skins under some conditions. He depends upon his skill, and that skill is nothing more complicated than an attitude which he sharpens up with a little practice. Here are some tips from the men who make a living by not dying at the wheel.

Skidding

Skids are fairly common at any speed on icy roads. You've seen them, and if everybody is rolling slow and keeping his distance the skidding car usually causes no damage. But not all skids are on icy roads, nor at slow speeds. Skids are possible when the slickness of the road is not obvious as a surface coated with polished ice. Some stretches of highway are slick when wet. Sometimes a thin coat of new snow covers glassy ice.

You control a skidding car by using three of your car controls in varying degrees. First is the steering wheel which you use hard. Don't be afraid to swing it fast to get the car under your control. Try to point your wheels in the direction you are skidding; this may call for rapid wheel work, as the very nature of a skid often has the car changing its own direction back and forth. Second, you use the throttle sparingly and judiciously. When the skid begins, ease up on the gas pedal but keep your foot right over it. When you feel you have the front wheels pointing in the direction you are skidding, apply a little gas and you should regain control of the car. The third item is your brake pedal which you do not use until you are absolutely in control of the car, and then you use it gently.

The worst handicap to handling a car in a skid is the nearness of obstructions, ditches, or other cars. If you find yourself skidding toward a collision or ditch it means you will need sharp skill and fast reflexes to get your car under control in time. It also means that if your point of control finds you heading into a collision, it will take an infinitely light touch on the throttle and wheel to turn your car away safely without going into another skid.

Sometimes a sudden skid at moderate or fast speed will turn your car around and send you sliding backward. A reverse skid is extremely difficult to control, especially as there is seldom the opportunity or room to put the transmission into reverse. Usually, about all you can do is try to get control of the steering until the car is rolling instead of skidding, then gentle the brakes. If you do have the time and the space to shift into reverse, you may be able to stop the car by the braking power of the motor. However, some automatic transmissions provide no braking power when the car is in gear. Looking over your shoulder and steering from the wrong end of a moving vehicle is mighty difficult. Just remember how you work the steering wheel when backing into a parking space, and manipulate the car accordingly.

Cornering

More rubber and dispositions are burned by kid-stuff drivers taking turns with squealing tires or brakes, or both. And more gas and brakes are applied wastefully by overcautious drivers who use more caution than skill when making sharp turns. The one booboo that is common to both the kid-stuff driver and the Sunday driver is using the throttle when he should use the brake and vice versa.

The sensible and safe method for turning a highway curve or a street corner is simple. You slow down as you *approach* the turn, shift down if necessary, then just as you go into the turn you apply gas lightly, increasing the gas as you begin the straightaway coming out of the turn. If you wait until you are actually into the turn before slowing down, you are inviting a screech, a skid, or a rollover.

If you have a long approach to the turn, you slow down by easing off the throttle until you get to the point where you begin to turn the wheels. If you come upon the curve suddenly, you will have to use your brakes. Don't slam them. On most cars you "play" the brakes, that is you press the pedal down, release it, press it down again, release it, repeating the process until you have the speed you need. On some vehicles you put your foot firmly on the brake pedal and squeeze it down gradually, not letting up until you are ready to apply gas.

As elementary as cornering should be, many inexperienced drivers have actually suffered accidents at speeds of less than 30 mph because they waited until they were actually into the turn before slowing down.

Blowout

The tire ads imply that blowouts can't happen nowadays, but still every new car comes equipped with a jack. True, a blowout is unusual on today's tires, but they still happen on occasion. And any time you hanker to liven up a conversation among two or more drivers, just pitch in the question: "Is a

Skids, Skins, and Skills

blowout on a front tire more dangerous than a blowout on a rear tire?"

One "expert" will tell you that a front blowout is worse because it messes up your steering control. Another will tell you the rear blowout is worse because it unequalizes the push in the driving wheels. Front or back, both experts will agree the blowout can be dangerous. At high speeds it can be deadly.

What do you do about a blowout? Well, you've heard the old gag about the directions on the medicine bottle that read "Take one spoonful *before* you feel the pain coming on." Before you get your blowout you put both hands on the steering wheel. No driver has yet had the roof of his car stolen while driving or a door whisked away by a playful breeze. So, take that protective left hand back in through the window and place it on the steering wheel. Now, when you hear the bang and feel the bump, here is what you do:

First you resist the impulse to shift your throttle foot over to the brake. You ease up on the gas, but not entirely, while you grip the wheel firmly, keeping the car traveling straight. When your speed has dropped sufficiently, pull over onto the shoulder, then brake to a stop.

You slow down gradually for two reasons: One, you maintain control of your car; if you slammed on the brake it could throw you into a skid. Two, you protect your rear from being rammed by the car following you.

The Sudden Obstruction

Accident reports are full of grief about "the little man who wasn't there" until one second before the collision. The car that suddenly shoots across the highway from a hidden crossroad, the joker who suddenly decides to make a left turn from the right lane, the cyclist or pedestrian who impulsively decides that the only time to come onto your road is right now.

This is the basic situation in most traffic accidents, yet it is a situation that rarely traps the race driver. On the track he always expects another car to suddenly skid in front of him, and he knows before it happens just what he will do. This attitude carries over into his street and highway driving.

When it happens to you, the first thing you do is honk your horn and apply your brakes. Hit both hard, but not so hard on the brakes that you lock the wheels and skid. At this point the cause of your emergency will hear your horn and brake noises and will most likely do something stupid. (Didn't he already pull one stupid stunt by tearing out in front of you?) You have a fraction of a second to analyze what he is doing, then you react accordingly. Here are the different situations and what you can usually expect from each:

Car crossing highway. If he has fully entered your right of way, the best he can do is to keep going, the worst is to stop. Either way you play your brakes and if you see you can't stop short of

Skids, Skins, and Skills 85

hitting him, try to find passing room to his rear—providing that won't bring you slam bang into another car driving on your right. If the accident-maker has stopped without completely obstructing the highway, make a fast estimate of the situation; see whether you can swerve left to pass in front of him without banging an oncoming car or sideswiping a car in the left lane.

Car cutting into your lane, traveling same direction. When he hears your horn the odds are the other driver will swing back into his own lane, allowing you to proceed. Some joker will do as he should have done five seconds earlier: he will flip on his turn signal and continue to bull his way into your lane. Keep playing your brake, then if necessary and if the road is clear, swerve out and around him.

Car coming head on. If it is in your lane you can figure the driver is either drunk, asleep, or having a heart attack. If you have passengers, yell at them to get down on the floor and hold their knees up toward their chests. Keep your horn blowing. In this situation be mighty careful with that brake; don't lock your wheels and don't get your car so slow that you won't be able to get out of the way. Do not try to pull out to the left; if he decides to change lanes at the same time you pull to the left, you are both dead. If you have to, drive off the road to the right. Don't be afraid to ditch. Ditching is less punishing than a head-on collision. If you can't get out of his way, at the last minute turn off your ignition and lie down on the seat, away from your steering wheel if possible, and draw your legs up. Now is an ideal time to wish you had your blood type recorded on your driver's license.

Cyclist. This is any man's guess. After he knows you are coming up on him, the cyclist may decide to do one thing but his bike may try to do something else. Be ready to swerve sharply past him either right or left, depending on which way he wobbles.

Pedestrian. You will usually be able to avoid the pedestrian by swerving in front of him. The average male pedestrian will either jump back at the sound of your horn, or freeze and let you avoid him. The average female will glare at you first, then dance back and forth—not quite sure which way to go. In either case, as long as you know the road is clear, your best move to avoid the pedestrian is by swinging in front.

No Brakes

One scary surprise about fluid brakes is that you can have tight, efficient brakes one moment, then suddenly have no brakes at all. It happens rarely, but if any leak in the brake system drains all the fluid out, you have no brakes. In such cases your parking or emergency brake is your margin of safety.

If you are ever caught completely without brakes, be resigned to ditch or bump your way to a stop. Try to shift your car into low gear. Pull over onto the shoulder if it is clear. If there is a guard rail, don't hesitate to bump the nearest upright with the edge of your bumper, then the next, then the next, and so on. Enough guard rails will bring you to a stop. You may wind up with the choice of hitting the guard rail hard or hitting other cars or people; your only real choice is the guard rail. On country roads, don't hesitate to hit small trees or hedges or embankments. If necessary, run into the ditch.

Headlight Glare

If the oncoming car is unwilling or unable to dim his lights, don't challenge him to a glare duel. Dim your own lights, slow down, and avoid looking at his lights. Guide your car by watching the white line and keeping your car on your side of the line. If the lanes are not marked, look to the right at the edge of the road and steer your car just inside the edge until brighteyes gets past.

The Skill Attitude

Now let's get back to that idea of taking the medicine "*before* you feel the pain coming on." In all the foregoing situations you would barely have sufficient time to concentrate on the immediate hazard. Your chances of avoiding disaster may depend upon whether you did take your medicine beforehand. That is, do you keep the big picture always in view (see Chapter 7) while driving, and do you know what your car will do under braking conditions?

There are still a few areas where, in winter, you can find a large body of water frozen over. If you are fortunate enough to live near such a place, drive out to it and practice handling your car in a skid. It's as much fun as ice boating and it pays dividends in driving skill.

You have a few things to check out before you zoom onto the ice. First, make sure the ice is thick enough to support your car. Second, see that you have lots of room to skid and swerve without mowing down skaters or fishermen or plowing into trees.

Drive your car onto the ice at about five miles per hour, not more than ten, then hit the brake hard. Now you're in a skid; get busy. After practicing this a few times, see whether you can put the car into a reverse skid. With a little practice you will learn just how much to turn your car before hitting the brake to get sliding backward. At first you will get spins that may end up with the car traveling sideways. Soon, however, by turning just enough you will be able to produce a reverse skid.

Not all cars react the same to brakes on normal road conditions. Practice emergency stops to determine how your car behaves. Find a stretch of empty road or use a large empty parking lot—a shopping plaza lot on a holiday, for instance. Get your car up to 15 or 20 mph then slam on the brakes. Learn at what point your wheels lock and which way they

Skids, Skins, and Skills   89

swing your car when they do lock. Test your brakes in this fashion on a straight run, then while making turns, both right and left.

Just one caution. Try to have an adult along when practicing, preferably a good driver. If you let the police know beforehand what you plan to do, and why—especially why—you can reasonably expect cooperation instead of interference, once they get over being amazed.

9. Had an Accident?

TRAFFIC ENGINEERS have not yet perfected the stop sign or signal device that will reach into the other driver's car and apply his brakes at the crucial moment. Scientists have long been making technical talk about electronic controls that will deflect one vehicle before it strikes another, but such devices are not operating yet. They are on the planning boards and we should see them in a future tomorrow, but that doesn't keep drivers out of courts and hospitals today.

Every driver on the road today runs a one-to-three gamble that he will be involved in some degree of automobile collision within the year. That is a possibility. If one driver is a teen-ager and his car does the striking, the average bystander will blame him.

Had An Accident?

That is a certainty. That is, the attitude of the bystanders is a certainty. The true blame? Well, it's something in the nature of the man who says, "I can't stand to argue with my wife because she is usually right."

If you are a male driver under the age of twenty-five you are in a statistical group that is responsible for more than its share of automobile accidents. Fortunately—and never forget this point—the law does not judge you by the statistics. The facts of each accident, and only the facts, will fix the blame, if any.

Regardless of whether you think you are blameless or know you are, it is wiser not to argue about fault at the scene of an accident. Argument can only get all parties excited at a time when there is already too much excitement or tension. Keep calm, and carefully and deliberately go through these steps:

1. *Shut off your ignition.*
2. *Do whatever you can to see that any persons who may have been injured get proper attention. (There is some instruction on elementary first aid at the end of this chapter.)*
3. *Check to make sure that neither car is left in a position where it might cause another accident. Try to get some disinterested party to warn off approaching cars while you and the other driver attend to your responsibilities. If necessary, you may have to move one*

or both vehicles out of the right of way.
4. *If the damage is more than a minor scraping, try to get someone to call the police. He—or you if you make the call—needs only to get to the nearest telephone and ask the operator for police headquarters.*
5. *Exchange car and driver information with the operator of the other vehicle.*
6. *Try to get the names and addresses of witnesses. Do this even if the other driver admits fault and assures you that your car will be repaired at no cost to you. If the fault is clearly yours, you will have less need for witnesses than you will have for liability insurance.*

When the police arrive keep cool and answer all questions briefly and correctly. Do not volunteer a long speech and don't try to argue your case. Don't get involved in challenging the statements of the other driver. All the police are required to do is write down three sets of facts: one, the details they see (such as which car is damaged and what is the nature of the damage); two, the facts you give them; and three, the facts the other driver gives them. They will take down the names and addresses of witnesses, but don't count on witnesses coming forward voluntarily. For your own protection, get out and ask all people in the vicinity whether they witnessed the accident.

From the other driver you will need the following information:

His full name and address.

The number of his license and the state in which he is licensed. Ask to see both his operator's license and the registration certificate (license) for the vehicle. If someone else is named as owner of his vehicle, get the owner's full name and address, as well as that of the driver. You need both the number on the license plate and the number on the registration certificate.

The make and year of the car, model (4-door, etc.), engine number, and serial number.

The name of the company on his liability insurance policy. (Be sure you get the liability *company, not his* collision *insurance company.) Get the number of his policy and address of the office where his policy is in effect.*

If the other driver fusses with you about writing down all this information, remind him that he is required by law to get the corresponding details from you and that both of you may have to file accident reports which must include that information.

Other facts you will need for making your accident report are: the names and addresses of occupants of either car who were injured; the date and time of the accident; the condition of the road (wet, slippery, dry, etc.). You will also need to know whether the scene of the accident was controlled by any stop signs, lights, or other traffic control. Get the correct name of the street or road; if an intersection, write down the names of both thoroughfares. Jot down the compass direction of each road.

Look closely at the other car before it is moved and write down the exact details of damage it incurred *in the accident*. If there are old dents or other signs of previous damage, make a note of them. It will be expensive enough for you or your insurance company to pay for damage you have caused, without getting stuck for damage you did not cause. If you carry a camera, take pictures of the other vehicle, showing the actual damage. If the scene, with the locations on which both cars ended up, seems to aid your cause, get pictures of it from different angles.

How Did It Happen?

Three interlocking factors make an automobile collision more complicated than "who hit whom?" *Fault, Responsibility,* and *Liability* may involve you in dealings with the driver and all occupants of both vehicles, with the police, with state motor vehicle officials, and with as many as four different insurance companies. This is one complexity of modern automobile economics that makes it unwise to be outspoken and say, "Sorry, buddy, my fault." It may be equally unwise to permit the other driver to up and say it was entirely his fault.

Some liability insurance policies will pay for damage done by your vehicle only when you give the insurance company enough of a toehold for a legal defense. If one driver voluntarily takes the driving responsibility for an accident, he may find his action gives his insurance company the right to just wash its hands of any financial responsibility.

That leaves the driver without liability insurance for his accident even though he holds a paid-up policy. If he doesn't have enough money to pay for the damage, then the other car owner actually suffers a loss because the first driver voluntarily accepted responsibility.

It is wiser, therefore, to make no statements about being at fault and to sign no papers submitted by the other driver (or by his insurance agent or his attorney) without first consulting your own insurance company. This is not a question of dishonesty, not a matter of denying your part in the accident. It is purely a matter of not substituting *voluntary* liability for your *legal* liability. When two moving vehicles collide, seldom is one driver completely at fault, regardless of how obvious the circumstances may seem.

Remember, therefore, if you are a driver involved in an accident, keep calm and do not be badgered into making any admissions that may cause you or the other driver some difficulties afterward.

About Insurance

Those four insurance companies which may be involved in the aftermath of your accident represent two for each driver. One policy is for "collision"; the other the "liability" insurance mentioned above. A collision policy is not compulsory, and if your car is more than six years old such a policy may not be advisable. The collision policy pays for the repairs to your vehicle, not the other car. Most policies are limited to the actual "book" value of your car—that is, the original price of the car when new, minus a depreciation based upon its age. Usually, you pay the first $50 for repairs; sometimes your policy requires you to pay the first $100. That means your policy is a "$50 deductible" (or $100 deductible), and you pay that much on each and every accident. All improvements and adornments on a customized vehicle will be disregarded, no matter how much you value them or how much money you have actually invested in those improvements and adornments.

If the other driver has a collision policy, that does not mean you are off the hook. His collision insurance company may come after you to regain the money it spends to repair his vehicle.

The liability policy is the insurance you carry to pay for any damage you cause to other cars or property or people. Liability insurance is required in most states. Those states which do not compel you to carry auto liability insurance may have laws which will make you sorry you did not have insurance should you ever become involved in an accident. In New York State, for instance, you must post a $250 bond, *no matter who was at fault* in the accident. Other states have liability laws just as tough or tougher. For instance, you might be sitting at a soda fountain with your car parked at the curb and become technically involved in an accident. If another vehicle hits your parked car, and either vehicle is sufficiently damaged to require the filing of an accident report, both drivers must establish financial responsibility. "Establishing financial responsibility" means that either you have a liability insurance policy or you post a cash bond.

If the damage to your car is to be paid for by the other driver's liability insurer it is probable that the insurance company will prefer to have its claim adjuster inspect your car before any repairs are made. Keep this possibility in mind if you need to have your car towed from the accident scene. Be sure you authorize *towing only,* and before you do so get a clear understanding of how much you will be charged for the towing. If the wrecker driver hands you a form to sign, insist upon reading it. If the circumstances—either a lot of small print on the form, or the driver rushing you—make it impractical to read it, then write across the face *I authorize towing only at no more than $——* and fill in the sum the driver quoted.

If the insurance company asks that you get two repair estimates from different repair shops, that is reasonable. Get the estimates to the company promptly and keep a copy or record of each estimate with all your other papers dealing with the accident.

Don't let any schnook talk you into "padding" the estimate. You hurt yourself when you ask for more money than the damage actually warrants. Insurance companies have reluctantly come to the conclusion that there is too much cheating on auto repair bills. Investigation of exaggerated claims is slow and expensive, and both the delay and the added cost are passed on to you and the rest of the insurance-paying public. Because of phony claims we all pay high for our insurance.

Even with a fair estimate you may have to allow the insurance company a week or ten days to get around to looking into your estimates or inspecting the car. If you are fortunate you may get action within one or two days. If you suspect the insurance company is stalling or otherwise being unfair, find out whether your state insurance department has a complaint bureau. Provided you have a just complaint you can ask the bureau how you can press your case.

If you must get your car back in running condition before the insurance company has settled with you, try to hold the repairs to exactly what you need for a safe-operating vehicle. Body repairs, usually the most expensive phase of the damage, can sometimes wait until the insurance company has seen either the car or the estimates. For those repairs that become necessary before you settle, ask the garage for receipted bills in duplicate. Submit one copy to the insurance company and keep the other. You can then make extra copies should the one you send to the insurance company get lost in the shuffle.

Once the insurance company (either your collision insurer of the other driver's liability company) agrees to pay for the repairs, the responsibility for getting an efficient job done is your own. Remember this point in getting your estimates. Select a reliable shop and when the work is done check off every detail against the estimate before you pay the bill. A good shop will stand behind its work, and if it develops within a day or so that some item has not been repaired correctly you will probably get satisfaction when you bring the car back.

If you have been injured in the accident you may find that the other driver's liability insurance company is unusually prompt and solicitous—perhaps more prompt than genuinely solicitous. The claim adjuster may be anxious to exchange autographs with you. He will be happy to sign a check for you if you will just sign a settlement for him. Don't be rushed. Wait until your doctor has determined the exact nature of your injury and until you know whether you may be expected to suffer any aftereffects. Neither you nor your parents should sign a claim release until you are sure of the total cost to you in medical bills and loss of earnings. Once you have determined those costs, then it may be wiser to come to an agreement with the adjuster than to go into court. Lawsuits are slow and expensive. The big court awards you hear about are exaggerated and are trimmed down considerably by legal expenses and appeals.

Thus, regardless of whether the fault is yours or the other driver's, you can be deprived of the use of your vehicle for any period from a few days to several months. You may find yourself forced to start all over again to save enough money to get a car. Once you have sweated out the reckoning up that follows an accident you will realize that careful, defensive driving is more than just another topic for a lecture.

Where Does it Hurt?

Statistics don't tell how many deaths have resulted because an injured person has, one, not received first aid; or two, been subjected to mishandling by an unqualified first-aider. Nor do the statistics tell how many patients died of hemorrhage, exposure, or just plain boredom while some would-be first-aider went through the frustration of trying to find the correct information in a first-aid manual.

What statistics do show is that of all people injured in an automobile accident, three out of every four suffer head wounds. Two out of every four casualties are injured in the foot or leg. Yes, that does add up to five out of four, and there are still four other body areas to be heard about. Actually, what this adds up to is that more often than not

Had An Accident?

a person injured in an automobile smashup is hurt in more than one part of his anatomy.

Here is the order of frequency in which injuries occur in the six general body areas: one, *head;* two, *lower extremities (legs and feet);* three, *thorax* and *thoracic spine (chest and upper spine);* four, *upper extremities (arms and hands);* five, *abdomen, pelvis, and lower spine;* and six, *neck and cervical spine.*

The following pages are about first aid. Actually, they advise you as much on what not to attempt to do, and spell out how to do the little you can do. Possibly the most important thing you can do for an injured person is what you do now, before you meet with an emergency. That something is to equip your car with a first-aid kit, including something you can use for splints, and read this section —or a more complete first-aid manual—today. It will help, too, if you mark the different first aid sections of this book where indicated with tabs and then carry the book in your glove compartment.

When you read the details on pressure points, check the body chart on page 102, and locate the different pressure points on your own person. Even if you do this only once, it may bury itself somewhere in your cranium and come back when you need to find certain pressure points on someone who is bleeding seriously.

When the time comes that you stand and look at an injured friend—or a stranger from the other vehicle—the first thing you must do is determine

PRESSURE POINTS OF THE BODY

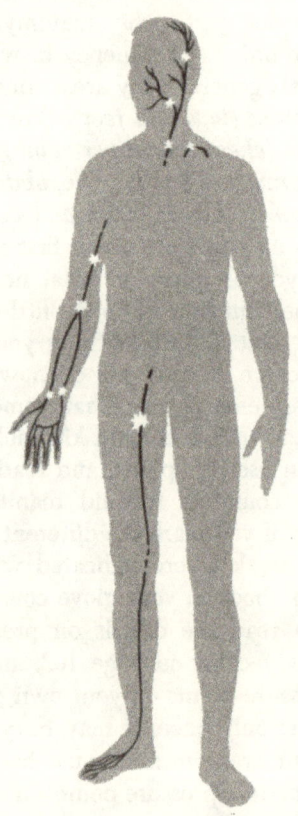

Knowing the location of pressure points in the human circulatory system is a large help in an emergency. Pressure points are marked above and described in the following text on the different body areas.

whether you are sure of yourself. If you don't know what to do or how to do it, *do nothing*. The wrong action is more dangerous than doing nothing. However, once you calm yourself down and take in the situation, you will realize that you can do something to prevent his injury from worsening.

First FIRST AID

Put DO FIRST
tab here

Send for help. Ask someone to call police or hospital or doctor. If the injured person is bleeding heavily, try to stop the bleeding. This is done either with a direct compress on the wound or by applying finger or hand pressure to the nearest pressure point. Specific details about locating pressure points are given in the paragraphs which deal with specific body areas.

A compress is a bandage or pad, preferably sterile, pressed directly on the wound. It can be held on the wound by hand or, if the injury permits, it can be fastened under a bandage.

Cover the patient to keep him warm. This helps to prevent or ease shock. Use extra garments from car passengers, blankets if available, car rugs, newspapers, beach towels, etc.

If the victim gets sick to his stomach, see that he is not in danger of swallowing the matter before he can get it out of his mouth. Turn his head gently to one side and, if possible, raise it so that he may vomit clear of his own person. A basin or any receptacle without sharp edges should be placed to catch the waste. If nothing else is available, a hubcap may do. Place a handkerchief or something soft between his face and the hubcap.

Do not move an injured person unless it is absolutely necessary—and absolutely necessary means only if letting him lie will certainly cause him worse injury. Cover him, try to protect him from the elements, and make him as comfortable as possible with as little movement as possible, but *do not move him* except when absolutely necessary.

Splints

Splints may be improvised from the following:

Boards or *slats*. Any reasonably straight lengths of wood, broomsticks, etc. Be sure wood is smooth or wrapped, with no nails or other projections which can make the patient uncomfortable.

Newspaper. Roll several pages tightly, lengthwise.

Bumper jack. Slide off the bumper support and wrap the upright so that the ridges on it do not make the limb uncomfortable. A bumper jack is a last choice because it is awkward to handle and is only a single splint. Splints are more reliable when used in pairs.

Remember that unless you are trained to handle injuries, there is just a little you can do. Do that little, then stop. Do not gamble someone else's life or limb on what you *guess* should be done.

Head

Put HEAD
tab here

See First FIRST AID on page 103.

A crack on the head can frighten bystanders worse than it hurts the patient. If the injury has opened the scalp there will most likely be copious bleeding. That will not be much indication of the extent of the injury, since the head bleeds profusely whether the laceration is minor or serious. On the other hand, a person who is unconscious or in a stupor may have had a severe bump on the head that is not obvious because hair hides the bump. If the head is not bleeding, the injury is not immediately obvious.

Any indication of a head injury should be treated as serious. Do not let the patient get up and walk around. Some people believe that a person who is groggy following a blow on the head should be made to walk around; this is wrong. It has been known to be deadly wrong. Let the victim lie quiet. Do not move him unless it is absolutely necessary to get him out of the car or off the road. Repeat: Do not move him unless it is absolutely necessary.

You can control bleeding of a head wound by applying pressure to one or two of six pressure points; there are only three locations you need to know, since the pressure points are paired on both sides of the head.

Bleeding from Scalp

Take your finger tips now and probe just in front of your ear, up almost level with your eye, until you feel the spot that is pulsing gently. This is the *temporal* artery, the one to which you apply pressure for scalp bleeding. In the event of profuse bleeding in one or more parts of the scalp it may be necessary to put pressure on the *temporal* arteries on both sides of the head.

Bleeding from Head

Probe with your fingers along the side of your neck, just above and forward of your collarbone. Here you should feel a pulsing a little stronger than in the case of the *temporal* artery. This is the *carotid,* and it controls the flow of blood to most of the head, including the upper part of the neck. It takes the thumb and two fingers to apply pressure. The thumb is placed behind the neck, and you press the other two fingers against the artery, squeezing it back toward the thumb. Be careful not to apply pressure to the windpipe. If your patient seems to be losing consciousness while you are applying pressure to the *carotid* artery, relax the pressure more frequently than normal for other pressure points. Do not continue pressure while the victim is unconscious.

Bleeding from Face

Run your finger tips along the upper rim of your

neck, to just below and forward of the point where your jawbone hinges. This is the *facial* artery; pressure here will control bleeding in the front of the face between under the eyes to the chin.

Leg and Foot

Put LEG & FOOT
tab here

See First FIRST AID on page 103.

It takes a severe gash to make the leg or foot lose much blood. Most injuries in the lower extremities will be a bruise, dislocation, or fracture. In a small percentage of severe injuries, feet or legs may be crushed or severed.

Bleeding of the leg or foot is controlled by heavy pressure on the *femoral* artery. The *femoral* artery is at the front of the leg, just immediately below where the thigh meets the torso. You apply pressure by pressing your fist or the heel of your hand firmly against the artery.

When the injury appears to be a fracture of the leg, there is not much an untrained first-aider can do. Make the patient comfortable without moving him. This may also mean gently restraining him if he is panicky and is struggling to move himself.

If you know it may be an exceptionally long time before any aid reaches you, or if other circumstances make it necessary, you may have to splint a simple leg fracture. Do *not* attempt to splint a compound fracture. (A fracture is compound when the bone is protruding through the skin or about to break through.)

When splinting a simple fracture it helps to have two people to do the job. Gently place the leg so that it is stretched out as naturally as possible. Do not apply pressure. Place small supports under the leg on both sides of the break, then lay your splints alongside the leg. Now straighten the leg by grasping the toe and heel and pulling gently. Keep the leg straight and supported until the splints are lashed firmly in place.

Chest and Upper Spine

Put CHEST & UPPER
SPINE tab here

See First FIRST AID on page 103.

The chest and spine are delicate areas in which little can be done by the first-aid man. Although only third in order of number of injuries due to auto accidents, this area, called "thorax and thoracic spine" by the medics, places second for fatal injuries.

Rib fractures are the most common type of chest injuries, but the most serious is the crushed chest. The steering column on the vehicle is held mostly to blame for a crushed chest, therefore this is the type of injury the driver might sustain.

The best you can do for someone suffering from an apparent chest or spine injury is to let him lie until the ambulance arrives. Try to keep yourself calm enough to remember that the chest protects the vital organs—heart, windpipe, lungs—and that broken bones can do damage to these organs if the patient is moved by untrained hands.

A jagged wound in the chest area may be a "sucking" wound, and as such is serious. A sucking wound may admit outside air to the space between the chest wall and lungs and cause the lungs to collapse. First aid for a jagged chest wound is to apply a large compress directly over the wound and hold it in place or secure it with a firm bandage. You must continue to take care that you do not worsen the injury should there be any broken bone fragments.

Injury to the spine is not always obvious, and sometimes may be overlooked by both the victim and others if the victim is also injured elsewhere. There have been cases where an injured person has been bundled into the back seat of another automobile to be taken to a doctor or hospital, and suffered paralysis because the automobile ride caused a broken spine to damage his spinal cord.

The possibility of severely worsening a spinal injury is one vital reason why no injured person should be moved by people who have not had medical or advanced first-aid training.

All you can do is keep the victim warm by covering with jackets, blankets, etc. Try to stop severe bleeding. If the patient is conscious, someone should stay beside him continuously until experienced medical help arrives.

Arms

Put ARMS
tab here

See First FIRST AID on page 103.

Injury to the arm is usually apparent, though the extent of injury may not be equally apparent. There are two pressure points at which you can apply finger pressure to stop excessive bleeding.

The *brachial* artery runs down the inside of the arm between the large muscles. The best point to apply pressure is midway between the shoulder and the elbow. Place your thumb against the outer side of the arm, and try to align your other four fingers along the artery and squeeze. If this does not work (a possibility when the wound is on the lower part of the arm), you may have to use a tourniquet. Pressure may also be applied immediately below the inner bend of the elbow.

Two arteries branch off the *brachial* at the elbow, travel down to the wrist, then branch off into the fingers. The *radial* artery courses down the thumb side of the inner arm and the *ulna* artery travels down the little finger side of the inner arm. You can usually see both arteries on the surface at the wrist and that is where you apply the pressure.

Do not attempt to splint a compound fracture of the arm.

Splint a simple fracture only if you know that competent medical help will not arrive within a reasonable time. If you have to splint a simple fracture, gently lay the arm in as natural a position as possible. Support both sides of the break by placing small pads underneath—such as wallets, books, rolled-up hats, etc. Put the splints in place, then gently straight the arm and hold it straight until the splints are firmly fastened in place.

Remember, never attempt to splint a compound fracture. Place a compress over it to stop the bleeding and keep it clean, then wait for trained medical personnel.

Abdomen Area

Put ABDOMEN AREA
tab here

See First FIRST AID on page 103.

Fortunately, the abdomen and pelvis are not often injured in vehicular accidents, for here again is a delicate body area. The first-aider can do little except make the patient comfortable until help arrives. You can stem the flow of blood with direct pressure with a compress on the wound. You can also try to keep the patient warm and relatively comfortable, assuring him that aid has been summoned.

Neck

Put NECK
tab here

See First FIRST AID on page 103.

Although the head suffers the most frequent injuries in automobile accidents, the neck has the lowest rate of the six body areas.

Bleeding from the neck can be controlled by pressure on the *carotid* artery; there is one on each side of the neck. The *carotid* artery is found low on the neck, just above and forward of the collarbone. You apply pressure by placing four fingers along the artery, and your thumb at the back of the neck.

A broken neck may be indicated when the patient is unable to move his head or fingers. Another indication may be an extremely weak finger grasp. You can move him only if the accident has left him in such a position that his neck is not properly supported. Using boards if nearby, or the nearest level stretch of road, lay the patient on his back. Remember, do not move unless absolutely necessary, and then it is equally necessary to transport him on a rigid support, flat on his back.

Final caution: When it comes to first aid, if you do not know what you are doing, don't do it.

10. Second Impact

THE HUMAN SKULL is no softie. We expose our heads to hot sun, then slosh icy water over them. We bang each other over the noggin with rolled-up magazines or newspapers, sometimes with objects not so flexible, and that's fun. The Scot uses his head for batting a rugby ball, and professional wrestlers butt their skulls against ring posts and fellow actors. A television private eye usually gets sapped two or three times within the twenty-six minutes of a thirty-minute program but he always comes through with the clearheaded thinking which traps the baddies in time for the final commercial.

Such horseplay with our skulls proves nothing medically. It does demonstrate that part of the public may accept the human head as being capable of absorbing terrific punishment. One segment of public that appeared to subscribe to the theory of the indestructible human head was the motor moguls of Detroit. Up to a few years ago their products provided unlimited opportunities for punishing your head. You got hard, unpadded dashboards, sun visors that would drop upon impact, solid steering wheels, and low, sharp-edged mirrors.

Most of us still drive cars with these booby traps built into them. If you are going to customize your own machine the odds are that you will buy a car more than five years old—the real old-fashioned meat-grinder model. If your family automobile is a late model it may now have a few safety improvements, but probably still sports a number of hard, jutting internal objects.

With these splendid opportunities the automobile provides, three out of every four of us who do get hurt in an automobile accident use our heads —to run interference. Of every forty persons injured in collisions, thirty get konked in the head; two of the thirty suffer fractured skulls, and one of the two dies.

Women in all age brackets somehow survive the automobile better than they survive household accidents and their various illnesses. All American men who survive their first quarter century will eventually die, but few of them will die because of automobile smashups. But not so the American species, male, aged fifteen to twenty-four. Nothing—no disease, no aggregation of household accidents, not even global war—will kill as many men under twenty-five as will gasoline buggy collisions.

The volume of accidents is senseless in itself. Worse, even if the number of accidents remains unchanged, it is doubly senseless to permit the killing and maiming they cause. The first impact of a car colliding does not spill blood. The second impact does. The cause of an automobile accident is one thing. The cause of injury is another. You could probably divide an atom as easily as you can divide the fraction of a second between the first and second impacts, but nonetheless it *can* be divided. What hurts you is not what the car hits or how fast it hits. Injury is caused when your body strikes a specific object. The severity of the injury is governed by the shape and hardness of the object and the force with which you hit it. This is the second impact, and you can not only separate it from the first impact, but you can also take a lot of the moxie out of its punch.

If you were shipping a $3.98 vase to your Aunt Hattie for Christmas you would have too much savvy to drop it loose inside a hard crate with a dozen jutting internal parts. You would never ship the vase in a carton with ends that pop open at the slightest pressure. Yet that is how you ship yourself and your date any time you ride to a dance or a basketball game, or just go spooking. That is how some of the family is shipped practically every day —to school, job, station, stores, or church. A new car arrives at the local dealer protected with more wrapping than the "wrapping" provided inside the car for you.

In the first fifty years of the automobile industry the only major safety factor to become standard equipment in all cars is the shatterproof windshield. Some cars have recently added one or more other safety features as standard equipment, and most cars can be equipped with other safety gear if the buyer is willing to pay more money. Unfortunately, with a mounting opposition to being stuck with a fat bill for "accessories," most customers are in no hurry to spend more money. Another reason for reluctance to add safety features is the prevailing erroneous opinion that they are a minor protection, and the deadly erroneous opinion that speed and speed alone is the big killer in automobile travel. And so we continue to get our heads battered in the almost unnecessary second impact of the inevitable collision.

While some of our heads are still functioning, let's knock out of them the false notion that smash-ups are the exclusive doings of speed demons and the luckless few drivers who get in the paths of the speeders. After collecting data for years from federal, state, local, and private agencies, the Bureau of Public Roads of the U. S. Department of Commerce recently came up with one fact that is a startling contradiction to the belief experts have held for some time. To wit: Most accidents occur at low speeds, not high speeds. For every accident at 65 mph there are six at 35 mph. On modern open highways the driver is reasonably safe at 55 mph, whereas the most dangerous speed is under 35 mph. But, before you ram your foot down on the throttle, hear this: The Bureau of Public Roads also established that the rate of death and injury in 65 mph accidents is more than double the death and injury rate in 35 mph accidents.

The average speed of cars involved in accidents that produce an injury is *41* mph at the moment of impact. The average speed of the vehicle just before the first impact becomes inevitable is *48* mph. In half of all accidents in which people have been injured, the vehicles were traveling at less than *40* mph when they hit other cars or stationary objects. Discouraging, isn't it?

The biggest discouragement is to us so-called "born drivers" who claim "automatic reflexes." If we are lucky we can hope to decrease the speed of the buggy by seven miles per hour before the bang.

At this point we can either accept the inevitability of an accident with the attitude that "what will be will be," or we can decide that the truck roadeo champ has the right solution. He's the driver who figures to make like a prize fighter and roll with the punch. This makes sense when you consider that accident researchers have established that how and where you sit in the car has more to do with whether you are injured than the speed of the car or the force of the first impact of the collision.

You can lose once at Russian roulette and you've

had it. You can lose at highway roulette and still be around for many more spins. There is plenty you can do to lessen the deadliness of that second impact.

First, you or the family have your own decision to make about the value of seat belts. The proseat-belters say the belt will keep you inside the vehicle when the door flies open, and that it will help prevent you from battering your face against the instrument panel and other blunt internal objects. The antiseat-belters say the belts can be a hazard. They point with alarm to one specific case of the overturned convertible. Two occupants wearing seat belts were dragged along the highway upside down, and what happened to their heads just wasn't pretty.

The antiseat-belters claim that if the occupants of the convertible had not been wearing seat belts they would have had a reasonable chance of being thrown clear of their car when it rolled over. It is also reported that some doctors wonder whether seat belts help cause abdominal injuries.

It may be true that had the occupants of the convertible not been wearing seat belts they might have been thrown clear of their overturned car. But statistics show that the most common cause of serious head injury is when people *are* thrown out of the car. Dragsters know this, and the official rules of the National Hot Rod Association say, in effect, that you wear a seat belt or you don't race. Here, specifically, is how the NHRA spells it out in their official rules:

> *Safety Belts:* All open bodied cars and all closed bodied cars having any body modification (i.e. chopped, channeled, gutted or sectioned) must be equipped with an approved quick-release type driver's safety belt in good condition. Belts must be securely fastened to frame, cross member, or suitable reinforced mounting by $5/16''$ minimum diameter bolts, in such a manner that all fittings are in a direct line with direction of pull. Steel castings of the type recommended by CAA, or "U" bolt type mounts are recommended. Flat metal plates, if used for attachment, must be a minimum of $¼''$ in thickness and have rounded edges to prevent cutting of safety belts. Under no circumstances will bolts inserted through belt webbing be acceptable for mounting.

Dragsters, you see, figure on being around for next season's race schedule. Note, too, that in spite of the furor about the overturned convertible, the National Hot Rod Association states positively that all open-bodied cars must be equipped with seat belts. The quick-release type of belt permits the driver to get out of his overturned car in a hurry if there is danger of fire.

One solid vote in favor of the seat belt comes

from Roy Campanella, one of baseball's most valuable catchers until he was paralyzed in an automobile upset. Less than a year after his crippling accident Roy was riding in the front seat of a sedan when a mobile air compressor broke loose from the truck which was hauling it. The compressor completely wrecked the front end of Campanella's car, but Roy was not hurt. "If I wasn't strapped in," he said, "I would have gone through the windshield."

Seat belts can be installed on any stock car or rod, and you can install them yourself, with one assistant. It usually takes two men because you may be working inside and under the vehicle at the same time. You must be positive that the belt itself and the method of anchoring it are both able to resist the pull of a person weighing up to 200 pounds. When you collide at normal road speed, a 200-pound body continues to travel at a force equal to 2,200 pounds or more. To get an idea of what that means, try a reverse mental picture: Imagine a 2,200-pound chunk of steel ramming into you. If your safety belt is properly hooked up and has sufficient tensile strength, it can spare you from being hit with as much as 3,000 pounds of force.

Your belt, therefore, should be heavy webbed material, approximately two inches wide, with a minimum tensile strength of 3,000 pounds. It must be lashed to a firm, nonmoving part of the car. If you attach the belt just to the seat itself, that means one more heavy object playing tennis with your head for a ball.

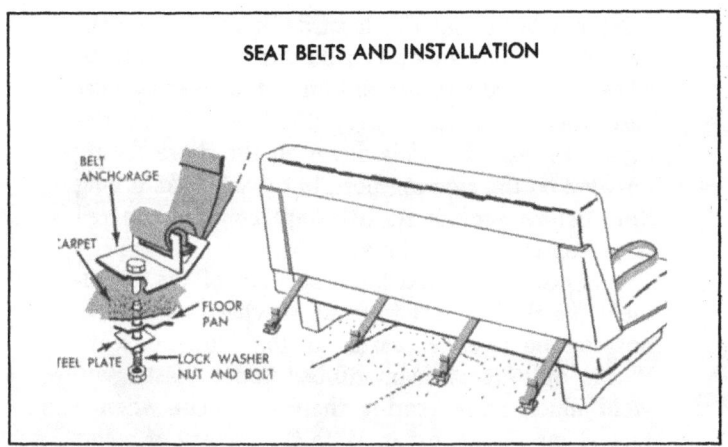

SEAT BELTS AND INSTALLATION

To anchor a seat belt properly in a street vehicle, each bolt runs through a belt anchorage fixture, car rug, floor pan, steel plate (or large washer), and then a nut. NHRA requirements are more rigid.

You can get safety belts through mail-order houses for between ten and fifteen dollars. Instructions with or on the package show you how to mount them by bolting the anchors through the floor of the car. If you can run the belt through the floor and bolt the anchor to the frame, your belt will be that much more secure.

The belt should come out of the floor to your hips at an angle of approximately forty-five degrees, and should be adjusted to fit on your lap, over the pelvis, with less than four inches of slack.

Next, what about the hazards of the instrument panel? Here, not much can be done for the driver, since the biggest threat to him is the steering post and wheel. The new "deep-dish" wheels are designed to take the odds down on the driver being impaled on the steering post, but it will take a long time before enough statistics are compiled to tell how well it is doing the job.

It is possible to pad the other half of the instrument panel, that part in front of what is known in hospital emergency wards as the "suicide seat." Plastic quilting or foam rubber under plastic will yield much more readily than steel will when a face slams up against it. With the variety of colors and patterns now available in plastic you may even carry the flames from a customized outer body right into the interior motif of your heap.

Close to three million people will be injured in automotive accidents this year. Over 40,000 will die. There are three positive steps you can take to increase your odds on keeping yourself out of these gruesome statistics. The first step is to be chicken—drive today with a firm intention of being around to drive tomorrow; reckless driving *is* kid stuff. The second step is to remodel the interior of your machine so as to reduce the wallop of that second impact. The third step is to learn first aid, a subject which has been ignored by the general public and left in the hands of the medics. And the medics are usually the last to arrive on the scene.

Second Impact

You may still be able to change the worst of your own driving habits, but few older drivers are going to be able to change. You can make the interior of your car less deadly to its occupants, and you can carry a first-aid kit in your car and know how to use it.

In short, don't lead with your skull. If the time comes when you can't duck fast enough, at least roll with the punch.

11. Tomorrow's Driving

THE WHEEL has dominated transportation since that prehistoric date when man first progressed beyond carrying himself and his few possessions on his own two feet. But tomorrow the wheel may be relegated to toys and museums. Vehicles that need no wheels and travel without touching ground are now in the working-model stage.

Pioneer models are open, bulky devices, given the technical designation of "ground effect machines." Popularly called air sleds because of their gliding performance, most of these machines are ungainly contraptions with one uncomfortable perch for the driver. In short, they are in about the same stage as the automobile was when it was a towering contraption powered by a steam boiler. But man is more advanced as a technician today than he was in the nineteenth century, and so we may look forward to a practical air sled within a year or two or three. Yours is the generation that will build them, then better them.

Whether the air sleds will replace all wheeled automobile is a moot question. Certainly they will replace feet and other conveyances for getting into places now accessible only to horses, airplanes, or boats.

The principle that propels the sled is simple. The engine sends a stream of compressed air blasting down toward the ground. The air cushion holds the vehicle a short distance above the surface and the vehicle slides on the cushion. The direction of movement is controlled by flaps in the air ducts or by auxiliary engines.

The army is interested in ground effect machines, and has encouraged their development. Both the army and the air force are also utilizing the same method of power for aircraft, which they describe as "vertical take off and landing," or VTOL. The helicopter has led to one of the first practical examples of the VTOL craft.

There are still some answers to be ferreted out before the air sled becomes a mass-production replacement for automobiles. For instance, engineers wonder whether the supporting air cushion can be sustained when the vehicle is pushed forward at rapid speeds. Climbing hills calls for a tremendous surge of power, perhaps more than can be built into a vehicle which is also expected to haul four to six passengers. Then there is the reaction which invariably follows an action: The blast of air that supports the sled off the ground also stirs up the dust and water underneath, either of which might become a serious hazard under heavy traffic conditions.

Until the air sleds do become practical, man in the meanwhile is planning highways and vehicles subject to controls that depend more on technology and less on the human factor. Engineers have finally admitted that the present-day automobile has one uncontrollable and dangerous working part—the nut that holds the steering wheel. Traffic and automotive engineers are now working toward highways with built-in radar that would be calibrated to prevent cars from colliding. Vehicles using the highway would, of course, have radar receivers and the driver, upon entering the highway, would flip a switch that would surrender much of the control of his car to a semiautomatic pilot which responds to the radar.

Two-car families of the future may find that instead of operating two similar vehicles, each car will have its special use. One will be designed for long-distance travel over turnpikes, the other built to serve best on short local trips.

The "highway cruiser" will probably be equipped with electronic and electromechanical devices that will either warn the driver about hazards or will slow down or turn the vehicle automatically. The car will be designed for safe and fast intercity transportation via a network of superhighways with fewer access roads than today's superhighway.

The future long-distance vehicle may have a rear engine to give it a flat floor and an aerodynamic shape. Windows, door handles, and trim will be flush and sealed. Most "highway cruisers" will be air-conditioned. All four wheels may be powered.

Passengers in the cruiser will probably sit as a sociable group, instead of all facing forward. Movable swivel seats will be designed to support the body comfortably and relaxed, and will probably be locked in place automatically whenever the brake is applied. Most cruisers will have domed, transparent roofs and will have ample room for six or more people.

Manual controls may still be necessary in some cars while they are traveling locally or to and from the superhighways. The steering wheel, however, will probably be replaced by a small lever which will activate power steering.

The engine and body of the car of the future will be made with metals lighter than those now being used. Aluminum, magnesium, and titanium are three light metals we know about today. Others will be developed by metallurgists who may graduate from college at the same time as you do.

Some stylists expect to use transparent material for structural strength above the frame. A new type of transparent material may be developed, one with all the present characteristics of glass, plus exceptional structural strength and reduced weight. Molded plastics may be used for panels subject to sideswiping or fender wrinkling. The majority of body surfaces that are not transparent may either have a permanent surface finish or permanent color incorporated into the material in its manufacture.

New Power Plants

What may be the first radical change in automobile engines was revealed publicly in 1959 by the famous airplane engine manufacturer, Curtiss-Wright. Working with the NSU Werke of West Germany, Curtiss-Wright has developed an internal combustion engine with only two moving parts. The makers call it a "rotating combustion" engine, and say that production will begin immediately on a unit with a range of 100 to 700 horsepower for passenger cars. A larger unit, not for automobiles, will be in the 750 to 5,000 horsepower range.

Compact and light, the rotating combustion engine has no valves, springs, camshafts, pistons, or connecting rods. The only two moving parts are a rotor inside the engine chamber, and the crankshaft.

An automotive carburetor supplies a mixture of gasoline and air into the rotating combustion engine's chamber through a side wall port. As the rotor turns, the mixture is compressed and fired by a single spark plug. The exploding gases power the crankshaft through the rotor. Exhaust is through another port in the chamber wall. Three power sequences per revolution to the crankshaft maintain an almost continuous intake, compression, ignition, expansion, and exhaust cycle.

Before the rotating combustion engine was announced, there were several experimental turbine-powered vehicles in operation. Trucks powered by gas turbine engines have been working out on proving grounds for a few years, and since the late 1950s a few experimental passenger cars have been making transcontinental runs.

Turbine engines for automobiles are similar to the engines on turboprop airplanes. They mix fuel and air (same principle as the piston engine), then ignite it, and the force of the expanding gas drives the vehicle. Engineers claim twice the efficiency for turbine engines over piston engines, especially at low speeds, where today's conventional engines are at their least efficient.

What kind of fuel will tomorrow's vehicles burn? That's a field that is really wide open. The wildest dreamers talk of an engine that contains its own permanent fuel, driving for the life of the engine without ever needing to replenish the fuel.

Permanent fuel may be for a distant tomorrow, but one possibility for the near future is that the impetus which rocketry and drag racing have given to the testing of different chemicals may result in a variety of inexpensive but efficient fuels. New engines, such as Curtiss-Wright's rotor combustion unit, will be easily adaptable to new fuels. The turbine engine will burn any fuel—literally meaning anything that will burn, including yesterday's newspaper. However, for many reasons, legal, logical, and otherwise, the turbines that power automobiles will burn standard liquid fuels stored in a fuel tank on the vehicle.

Batteries that pack more juice for longer periods will soon be on cars. The present lead-and-acid batteries will give way to nickel-cadmium power packs, similar to the huge batteries now used on diesel-electric trains. The success of these batteries has already started a few manufacturers back in the business of making—and selling—cars powered by electricity.

Bearings made of indestructible plastic are now being tested on some vehicles. Plastic bearings are expected to last the full life of the vehicle, and never need greasing.

"Transaxles" are now being manufacured and any year now they may be standard automobile equipment. By using transaxles, engineers will be able to build the transmission into or near the rear axle and thus reduce the hump down the center of the auto floor.

Fuel tanks in a few years from now most likely will be plastic and will be built into locations on the vehicle that otherwise would be waste space.

Dream stuff? Well, every possibility mentioned so far in this chapter is based upon developments and theories which have been tested. Some have been actually demonstrated. There are many reasons why we don't get these new inventions and improvements overnight. One is cost. The production engineers must first devise a method of making them in quantity and inexpensively. Another is the bulk of the working parts. Pioneer models are usually large and unwieldy. Every part must be engineered down to practical operating size before the device can be put into everyday use.

One dream we are not likely to ever see realized is an atom-powered automobile; not unless there is a new departure in handling atomic fuel that is as revolutionary as splitting the atom was. The big "Nix" is because of the threat to contamination should an atom-powered automobile be wrecked. Another serious obstacle is that the shield necessary for the reactor would be bulky and heavy.

Engineers are now testing sections of pavement with electronic controls installed along the roadside. These controls monitor cars on the highway and when one gets dangerously close to another, or runs through a warning signal, the controls beam a signal that applies the car's power brakes or operates its power steering. Since all cars using superhighways at that time will have automatic transmissions, electronic impulses will not be needed to shut off the ignition. Applying the brakes will stop the vehicle.

So far, working models of such electronic devices can prevent one car overtaking and ramming another. Whether they can be perfected to avoid head-on collisions is one question that keeps the electronicist from getting bored. As far as stopping broadside collisions at an intersection, no one has yet ventured the hope that electronics can do it—"more cloverleaf intersections" is the near-unanimous answer.

When your father learned to drive there was only a fraction of the number of cars on the roads as compared with today, but the blowout was more or less common. When your son learns to drive, say "blowout" to him and he may have to look the word up in the dictionary. Tubeless tires and self-sealing tires are already old hat, but they are not completely blowout-proof. Tire makers are now experimenting with foam-filled tires. Tests with urethane foam already promise tires that will never blow out.

Safer highways, safer cars, and safer tires, but what about the driver? The scientists are studying him closely, too. They have quite a book of facts on him, most of them dealing with his "hidden anxieties," "predisposing influences," "physical environments," and other psychological classifications. Some other facts in the book are pretty plain and nontechnical, such as one fact that jolted the Defense Department into contributing a large sum of taxpayers' money into accident research programs. That fact was that teen-agers in the armed services have five times as many accidents as the average for civilian drivers of all ages. During our last war (Korea) more servicemen died on American highways than died in combat.

On the brighter side of the ledger are the exciting places and adventures the future cars and highways will open up for all of us. In nineteen-eighty-anything it will be a snap to drive your family on a transcontinental tour during a two-week vacation. If you have three or four weeks—which will probably be the standard vacation period by then—you will be able to tour the country leisurely.

It's going to be worth sticking around.

Appendix I. Dragging Jargon

Bring together two or more people who are interested in the same activity and the first thing they will do is organize a club. The second thing they will do is coin a new language. In the world of automobiles there are at least two such "languages." There is one for the men who build and service cars, and one for the hot-rodders who rebuild them. Since words from both languages have just naturally crept into this book, and since you may meet with drivers and mechanics who lapse into their strange tongues, this glossary has been included. You may find it necessary every now and then to look back here for some English translations.

Ammeter: A measuring device to determine the strength of electric current moving through a circuit. Current must continue *through* the ammeter, not terminate in it.

Bent eight: Vehicle with eight-cylinder V engine.

Binders: Brakes.

Blowby: Particles of carbon and exhaust gases that blow by the piston rings and enter the crankcase instead of being carried out the exhaust system.

Blue dots: Purple taillights.

Bomb: One of many names for a hot rod.

Bullnosing: Replacing hood ornaments with low, smooth metal strip. Strip may be bought via mail order to fit practically any model car.

Carb: Short for carburetor.

Channeling: Lowering body of car to bring it closer to ground.

Chopping: Cutting sections out of windshield posts and center posts to lower vehicle's roof.

Combustion cycle: The four strokes a piston goes through when the engine is operating.

Competition disc: Flat, smooth hubcap for racing car.

Appendix I, Dragging Jargon

Compression ratio: The degree to which the compression stroke compresses the fuel-air mixture; i.e., a 10:1 compression ratio means the mixture is squeezed into a pocket one-tenth the total area of the cylinder.

Continental kit: Metal compartment mounted on trunk of vehicle to hold the spare tire. Sometimes a dummy addition that cannot house a tire.

Cornering: A car that holds firmly to the road, turning fast, without swaying or leaning noticeably, is good at cornering.

Crown (as in crown of road): A high center usually built into narrow roads to provide drainage.

Customizing: Changing the silhouette and trim of a stock car.

Dash-pot: Device on some stock cars that keeps throttle from closing fast and stalling engine when foot is lifted suddenly off gas pedal.

Deuce: A 1932 Ford. Often considered the ideal stock car for converting into a drag racer.

Diegoing: Replacing front axle with one especially designed to lower front end of car.

Double shocking: Adding a second shock absorber, or replacing a single shock with two.

Drag or dragging: A race to get to the fastest possible speed per hour over a quarter-mile distance from a standing start.

Draggin' wagon: Automobile rebuilt primarily for drag racing. Any hot rod.

Dropping: Same as channeling.

Duals: Exhaust system with two tail pipes.

Fireplace: Front grille.

Flame thrower: Souped-up ignition system.

Flames: Contrasting colors painted on body of vehicle.

Flippers: Hubcaps.

Four banger: Four-cylinder engine.

Frenching: Fitting hoods over headlights to give them the appearance of being recessed.

Full house: Engine with maximum souping up.

Full race: Engine tuned especially for drag racing, and thus with a tendency to stall at ordinary street speeds.

Appendix I, Dragging Jargon

Glass packs: Packing muffler with fiber glass to give it a powerful roar.

Glassing: Filling body holes with lead, compound, or fiber glass. Usually done after removing chrome.

Goodies: Fancy body ornaments.

Grease monkey: Garage or shop employee who does unskilled chores. Good apprenticeship training for a would-be mechanic.

Gutting: Removing interior metal, panels, upholstery, etc.

Hack: A hot rod.

Head: Top surface of engine block. Can be removed to service cylinders, pistons, etc.

Headers: Pipes used for leading exhaust directly out of cylinders without going through muffler.

Hides: Tires.

Hollywoods: Fancy exhaust system.

Johnson rod: There is no such rod. When you can't figure out what's ailing your engine, you blame it on the Johnson rod.

Jug: Carburetor.

Leading: Same as glassing.

Leaner jet: A leaner-than-standard jet for carburetors of cars that may be expected to spend most of their days in high-altitude country.

Louvering: Long narrow cuts in the hood for cooling the engine.

Machine: A hot rod. Any automobile.

Mill: An auto engine.

Moon: Hubcap.

Nerf bar: Bumper.

Nosing: Same as bullnosing.

Odometer: The instrument that records the total number of miles the vehicle has been driven.

Pin striping: Painting narrow stripes at handles and other parts of car body.

Pipes: Fancy exhaust system.

Posts: Upright members of car body at both ends of windshield and between each pair of doors on four-door vehicle.

Appendix I, Dragging Jargon

Pot: Carburetor.

Rag top: Convertible.

Rail job: Vehicle fully customized for drag racing.

Raking: Same as diegoing.

Screamer: A hot rod.

Shaving: Removing body trim preliminary to customizing.

Skinning: Removing car's upholstery (usually to replace with flashy new material).

Skins: Tires.

Sleeper: Car with more power than you would suspect by looking at it.

Slick or Slicker: Oversize tire for better traction. Usually wide and flattened where it contacts the road.

Slingshot: Car rebuilt solely for drag racing.

Slug: Piston.

Slush car: Vehicle with automatic transmission.

Smitty: Same as glass pack.

Snowball: White-wall tire.

Spaghetti: Too much chrome.

Spinner: Flashy hubcap.

Spooking: Just out for a drive; no particular destination.

Squirrel: The type who guns his motor and burns his tires.

Stacks: Fancy exhaust.

Stick car: Vehicle with standard clutch transmission.

Stock: The car just as it was built by manufacturer.

Stormer: A hot rod.

Strides: Expendable pants or dungarees worn while doing the messy work of customizing.

Striping: Same as pin striping.

Stripping: Same as shaving.

Stromberg: Special step-up carburetor made for racing vehicles.

Appendix I, Dragging Jargon 143

Tail-gating: Driving recklessly close to rear of another vehicle.

Tails: Fox or coon tails tied to vehicle.

Thingie: Vehicle souped up for drag racing.

Three-quarter race: Souped-up car that may also be used for normal street driving.

Top end: Highest speed that can be squeezed out of the car.

Trumpets: Extensions on tail pipes.

Uncle Daniel: Same as sleeper.

Velocity stacks: Air funnels on carburetors which eliminate cleaners.

Z-ing: Lowering car by cutting notches in frame.

Appendix II. What Makes it Go?

"Everyone is an expert on what makes his car go," observes the auto mechanic, "but when the car stops going, he comes to me. I'm the expert on what makes it *not* go."

What does make your car go is the engine. Many other working parts are important—wheels, for instance—but let's concede that the power that turns the wheels is the "what" that makes the car go.

The engine in your car is a four-cycle internal-combustion engine. It is started in operation by energy stored in a battery, and once it gets working, the engine propels the car, gives the battery back the energy used to start it plus more energy to fire the spark plugs, burn the lights, and operate the various electric accessories.

"Internal combustion" means that the fuel is

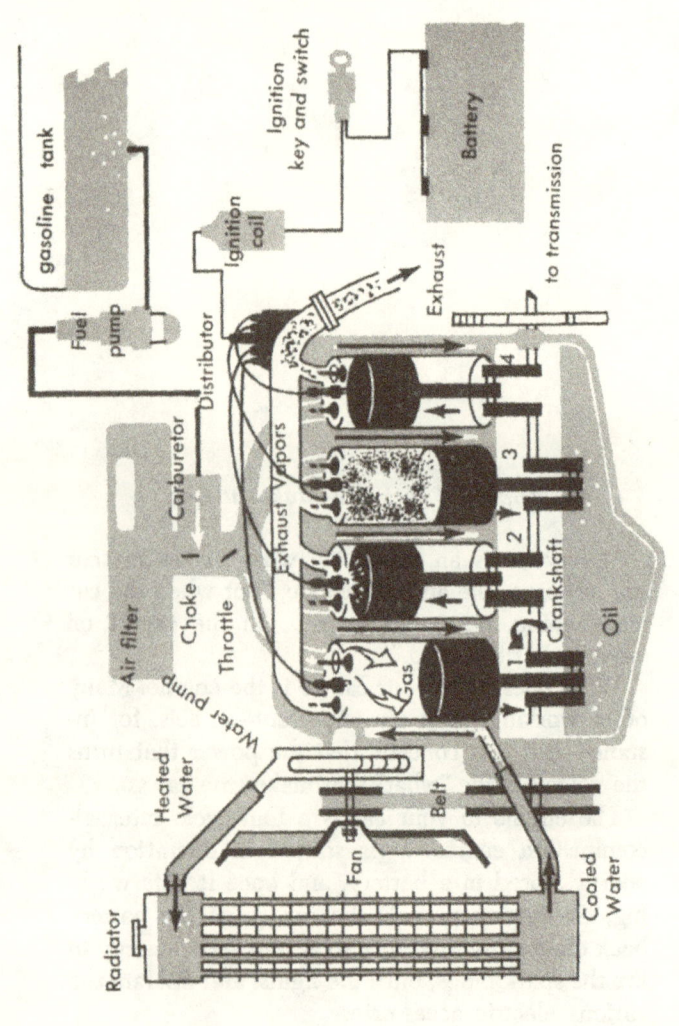

Appendix II, What Makes It Go? 147

burned *inside* the working engine, rather than outside (such as in the case of an engine powered by a steam boiler). "Four-cycle" is actually a shortened expression for four-stroke-cycle, and means that each piston in the engine operates on a cycle of four different strokes, two up and two down.

To make the pistons operate their four strokes efficiently there are several mechanical, electrical, and vacuum parts attached to the engine itself by wires, hoses, or metal connections. These are:

The **battery,** which supplies the initial electrical power and powers the accessories and spark plugs with energy which is replenished by the

Generator, a miniature power house that produces electricity similar to the way it is produced by the huge hydroelectric plants. Instead of harnessing a surging river, your auto generator takes energy from the engine's crankshaft, via the fanbelt. The fanbelt also operates the

Cooling system. The cooling system is comprised of a fan, a radiator, and a water pump. The fanbelt turns the fan and operates the water pump. The pump sends hot water out of the water jacket (which is the inside lining of the engine block) through the upper hose into the radiator. The water trickles through myriad channels in the radiator and is cooled by the fan. The cooled water is then drawn through the lower hose back into the water jacket. ("Cool" is a relative term here. The water from the radiator is usually between 100 and 190 degrees.)

Ignition coil, usually referred to merely as "coil." This is a sort of transformer. It takes the six or twelve volts from the battery and steps them up to approximately 20,000 volts.

The **distributor** is the electrical timing device which feeds juice to the spark plugs one at a time in the right order. The heart of the distributor is the breaker points, usually called "points."

The **air cleaner** is the big bowl that sits on top of the engine. It filters the air which is sucked through it into the

Carburetor, a gadget which provides you with 94 per cent of your fuel free. This it does by mixing 15 parts of air (by weight) with 1 part gasoline. By volume the difference is even greater—9,000 cubic feet of air to 1 cubic foot of gasoline.

The **fuel pump** draws the gasoline through the gas line out of the gas tank and into the carburetor. It is attached between the carburetor and the

Settling bowl, which draws the impurities out of the gas before it goes through the fuel pump.

The **oil filter** cleans the particles of metal and other garbage out of the oil bath which lubricates the pistons.

The **dip stick** is what you use to measure the quantity of oil in the engine block.

The **oil refill** is a capped opening into which oil is added when the dip stick shows it is needed.

The **spark plugs.** A spark plug is a porcelain insulator wrapped around a wire electrode which runs vertically down the center. At the bottom of

Appendix II, What Makes It Go?   149

the plug a steel shell is wrapped around the insulator, threaded at the bottom so it may be screwed into the spark plug opening on the engine block. Attached to the bottom of the threaded shell is another electrode which is bent inward to come within a few thousandths of an inch from the tip of the center electrode. When the spark plug gets a charge of juice from the distributor, a spark jumps from the center electrode to the bent electrode, and that spark ignites the fuel mixture in the cylinder.

In addition to visible parts, there are several functioning devices inside the engine block. They are:

Cylinders, or combustion chambers, each containing a

Piston, which fits snugly within the cylinder wall, but occupies less than half the top to bottom space.

A **connecting rod,** one end of which is fitted to the bottom of each piston. The bottom of the rod connects to the

Crankshaft. The crankshaft is a series of cranks shaped like U's. One connecting rod fits to the horizontal bar of each crank.

Flywheel. A double-purpose device, the flywheel is attached to the end of the crankshaft. Its momentum helps keep the crankshaft turning at a consistent speed. The flywheel is also turned over by the starter, and in turn starts the engine operating.

Timing gears are two gear-toothed wheels. The smaller wheel is attached to the crankshaft and is geared into the larger wheel, which fits the

Camshaft. The camshaft turns at half the speed of the crankshaft, and serves to open the valves in their proper rotation.

Valves come in pairs for each cylinder. One is the intake valve, which opens to admit the fuel and air mixture into the cylinder. The other is the exhaust valve, which opens to permit the exhaust to be driven out of the cylinder.

There are other working and anchoring parts inside and outside the block, but those described so far are the main functioning parts. Now, here is how your engine works from the moment you sit at the steering wheel and put the transmission in neutral.

When you turn the key in the ignition switch you start a flow of electricity from the battery through the coil to the distributor. Next you activate the starter; in most vehicles that means you turn the ignition key a little beyond the point where it turned on the ignition. In some cars and trucks you have a separate starter button on the floor or dashboard or built into the gas pedal.

The starter operates an electric motor which spins the flywheel, and the flywheel turns the engine over. Once the engine is started, the main function of the ignition system is to deliver the electricity to keep it going. Here is how:

Power originates at six or twelve volts in the battery, is stepped up to the vicinity of 20,000 volts

Appendix II, What Makes It Go?

at the coil, then enters the distributor. The distributor sends a charge to each spark plug in a predetermined rotation. This brings us to the engine cycle. The four strokes in the engine cycle are intake, compression, power, and exhaust.

1. **Intake.** On the *intake* stroke the piston drops down toward the bottom of the cylinder, sucking in the fuel and air mixture into the cylinder (or combustion chamber).

2. **Compression.** When the piston reaches the bottom of the cylinder it starts up on the *compression* stroke. The intake valve at the top closes and the fuel mixture is compressed at the top of the cylinder. (The space into which it is compressed is known as the compression ratio of your engine. For example, if the mixture is packed into one-eighth the full capacity of the cylinder, then the compression ratio is 8 to 1.)

3. **Power.** As the piston reaches the top of the compression stroke, the spark plug ignites the compressed mixture and slams the piston down to the bottom again. That is the *power* stroke.

4. **Exhaust.** On the *exhaust* stroke the piston travels up the cylinder again, crowding the waste gases out through the exhaust valve. When the piston reaches the top and has forced out all or most of the exhaust gases, the piston is in position to begin the cycle over again.

It is the power stroke that turns the crankshaft. Regardless of how many cylinders in the engine, the crankshaft makes two full revolutions in a cycle in which all pistons go through their four strokes. The larger the number of pistons, the more force being used to make those two turns of the crankshaft. The crankshaft is harnessed to the rear wheels, via the transmission, and "that's what makes it go."

Index

accident first aid, 100-112
accident, proportion to young drivers, 4
accident, relation of speed to, 116-117
accident, reporting, 93-94
accident, what to do in case of, 91-93
all-seeing eye, developing, 75-76
American Trucking Associations, 51
auto maintenance, periodic, 57-61
automotive engineers, 38

batteries, new types of, 130
blowout, 82-83
body job, the 31-36
booby trap, avoiding, 76

"book value" insurance, 36
boring, 41
braking distances, 67-68
bullets, 36
bullnosing, 34
bumper jockey, 69
Bureau of Public Roads, 116

Campanella, Roy, 120
carburetor, dual-barrel, 28
carburetor, four-barrel, 28
car crossing highway, 84-85
car cutting into your lane, 85
cars of the future, 126-127
choke heater, 31
Chrysler Corporation, 51
compression ratio, 21
continental tire, deck, 35

cooling system, draining, 25
cornering, 81-82
crankcase replacement plugs, 30
Curtiss-Wright, 128
cyclist, 86

decals, 35
Detroit, 18, 38
Dowguard, 25
drag racers, classes of, 48-49
drag racing, 19
drag strip course length, 47
drag strip insurance, 47
"drop the dollar," 66-67

engine, principle of, 54
engine, rotating combustion 128
exhausts, dual, 29-30
exhausts, multiple, 44

fan hub, freewheeling, 31
fender skirts, 35
first aid
    abdomen area, 111
    arms, 110-111
    chest and upper spine, 108-109
    head, 105-107
    leg and foot, 107-108
    neck, 111-112
flames, 34
foreign cars, parts for, 16-17
"fringe vision," 74

fuel injectors, 45
fuel pump magnetic trap, 30
fuels, future, 129

glossary, 135-143
ground effect machines, 124

headers, 44-45
head, high compression, 21
head injuries in collisions, 114
headlight glare, 87
head, milling, 21
head on, car coming, 85-86
head, removing, 25-26
hot rod, average, 18
humidifying air breather, 31

ice, driving on, 88
Indianapolis, 38
insurance, complexities of, 95-100
insurance, deductible, 96
insurance, drag strip, 47
insurance, liability, 96-97
insurance, liability, rates to young drivers, 4-5

Jaycees, 51-52

knowing what's up ahead, 75

Le Mans, 38

Liberty Mutual Insurance
  Company, 51
louvers, 35
lowering, stock kits, 32

manifolds, adding, 44
Mantle, Mickey, 68
Montgomery Ward, 34
muffler, packed, 30
multi-carburetion, 28-29,
  43

National Hot Rod
  Association, 47, 50, 119
National Truck Roadeo, 70
noises, car, 62-63

oil filter, 56-57
oil filter, changing, 27
oil filters, types of, 27, 57

pedestrian, 86
points, dual, 31
polishing, 40
porting, 28, 39
pressure points, 102
Pure Oil Company, 51

race drivers, 78
radar, highways with built-
  in, 126
rail job, 18
rear end, lowering, 31-33
relieving, 39

Santa Ana, Calif., 46
Sears, Roebuck, 34

seat belts, 118
  NHRA requirements, 119
  tensile strength, 120
secretive, how not to be,
  76-77
skidding, 79-81
skill attitude, the, 87-89
spark plug gap gauge, 26
spark plugs, cleaning, 26
spark plugs, when to
  change, 55
spinners, 35
splints, 104
steering habits, correcting,
  74
stripping, 34
stroking, 42
sudden obstruction, the 84
superchargers, 45

Teen-Age Road-e-o, 51-52,
  72
Teen-Age Road-e-o
  Committee, address of, 52
testing used car, 10-16
transaxles, 130

U.S. Junior Chamber of
  Commerce, 51-52
used car, buying, 9-17

velocity stacks, 44
VTOL craft, 125

"watching the big picture,"
  69, 75
wheel discs, 35

Z-ing (the frame), 32-33

www.ingramcontent.com/pod-product-compliance
Lightning Source LLC
LaVergne TN
LVHW091259080426
835510LV00007B/323